German Pronunciation : Practice and Theory

Viëtor, Wilhelm

Copyright © BiblioLife, LLC

BiblioLife Reproduction Series: Our goal at BiblioLife is to help readers, educators and researchers by bringing back in print hard-to-find original publications at a reasonable price and, at the same time, preserve the legacy of literary history. The following book represents an authentic reproduction of the text as printed by the original publisher and may contain prior copyright references. While we have attempted to accurately maintain the integrity of the original work(s), from time to time there are problems with the original book scan that may result in minor errors in the reproduction, including imperfections such as missing and blurred pages, poor pictures, markings and other reproduction issues beyond our control. Because this work is culturally important, we have made it available as a part of our commitment to protecting, preserving and promoting the world's literature.

All of our books are in the "public domain" and some are derived from Open Source projects dedicated to digitizing historic literature. We believe that when we undertake the difficult task of re-creating them as attractive, readable and affordable books, we further the mutual goal of sharing these works with a larger audience. A portion of BiblioLife profits go back to Open Source projects in the form of a donation to the groups that do this important work around the world. If you would like to make a donation to these worthy Open Source projects, or would just like to get more information about these important initiatives, please visit www.bibliolife.com/opensource.

GERMAN PRONUNCIATION:

PRACTICE AND THEORY.

*THE BEST GERMAN — GERMAN SOUNDS, AND HOW THEY
ARE REPRESENTED IN SPELLING — THE LETTERS OF
THE ALPHABET, AND THEIR PHONETIC VALUES — GERMAN
ACCENT — SPECIMENS.*

BY

WILHELM VIËTOR,

PH. D., M. A. (MARBURG),

PROFESSOR OF ENGLISH PHILOLOGY, MARBURG UNIVERSITY; FORMERLY
LECTURER ON TEUTONIC LANGUAGES, UNIVERSITY COLLEGE,
LIVERPOOL.

FIFTH EDITION, REVISED.

LEIPZIG.
O. R. REISLAND.
1913.

PREFACE TO THE FIRST EDITION.

There are two opinions frequently expressed with regard to German pronunciation, the one directly opposed to the other. People who know very little about it generally think it easy enough to acquire a correct German pronunciation from the ordinary spelling and the indications contained in any German school grammar, or, at all events, with the aid of a native, if possible Hanoverian, teacher. Those who have looked into the matter more closely are, on the contrary, inclined to consider it a hopeless task to try to arrive at reliable results, where there seems to be nothing but uncertainty and contradiction amongst the Germans themselves. In the following pages I have endeavoured to show that neither of these views is correct, but that, with some care and good will, a standard German pronunciation may indeed be pointed out to, and acquired by, English learners of our language. Readers who wish for fuller information as to phonetic and dialectal peculiarities, and the history of Modern German sounds, I beg to refer to my *Elemente der Phonetik und Orthoepie des Deutschen, Englischen und Französischen* (Heilbronn: Gebr. Henninger, 1884),[1] in which due regard has been paid to the works of the leading English phoneticians, Messrs. A. J. Ellis, A. M. Bell, H. Sweet, and W. R. Evans. The pronunciation of about 2,400 German words, indicated by means of the sound-notation used in the present little volume, will be found in a pamphlet which I am preparing for the press: *Die Aussprache der in dem "Wörterverzeichnis für die deutsche Rechtschreibung zum Gebrauch in den preufsischen Schulen" enthaltenen Wörter* (same publishers).[2]

The German spelling adopted here is that given in the official Rules and Word-list for Prussian schools.

I have to thank Mr. W. B. Evans, of London, and Herr F. Franke, of Sorau, for the kind and valuable assistance they have rendered me in the revision of the proof-sheets.

MARBURG A/L., *October* 1884.

---

[1] Sixth edition in the press. Leipzig: O. R. Reisland.
[2] Eighth edition: *Die Aussprache des Schriftdeutschen.* Mit dem "Wörterverzeichnis für die deutsche Rechtschreibung zum Gebrauch in den preufsischen Schulen" in phonetischer Umschrift sowie phonetischen Texten. Leipzig: O. R. Reisland, 1911.

PREFACE TO THE SECOND EDITION.

WHILST the general plan of this little book remains unaltered in the present edition, I have taken advantage of this opportunity to introduce a number of minor improvements and corrections, not a few of which are due to the valuable observations contributed by Miss Laura Soames, of Brighton, who has kindly read the proof-sheets.

The chapter on German Accent has been re-written and considerably enlarged, on the lines followed in the corresponding chapter of the Dutch edition (*De Uitspraak van het Hoogduitsch. Voor Nederlanders bewerkt door* W. Viëtor and T. G. G. Valette. Haarlem: De Erven F. Bohn, 1889),[1] where the subject is treated still more elaborately.

MARBURG A/L., *October* 1890.

---

[1] Second edition, 1902.

PREFACE TO THE THIRD EDITION.

IN the present third edition the text of this book has again been revised and partly rewritten. The German spelling is the new official one of 1902, the phonetic notation that of the *Association Phonétique Internationale* (as employed in *Le Maître Phonétique*, edited by Dr. Paul Passy, 20 rue de la Madeleine, Bourg-la-Reine, France). For a number of corrections I am indebted to Dr. E. R. Edwards, of the University of London, who has kindly assisted me in seeing this new edition through the press.

MARBURG A/L., *August* 1903.

PREFACE TO THE FIFTH EDITION.

THE fourth edition (1909) did not call for any special remarks. I have taken the opportunity offered by the present reprint in order to introduce further corrections, and to supply the List of Symbols which had inadvertently been omitted in the two previous editions. Most of the misprints, &c., now corrected were kindly pointed out to me by Mr. R. H. Cheatle, Prof. D. L. Savory, Fräulein M. Taubner, and Mr. H. B. Walker.

MARBURG A/L., *September* 1912.

W. VIËTOR.

CONTENTS.

	Page
Prefaces	I
List of Symbols	VIII
The Best German	1
German Sounds, and how they are Represented in Spelling	7
1. Vowels	7
Front Vowels	8
Back Vowels	21
Mixed Vowels	30
Diphthongs	32
Nasal Vowels	35
2. Consonants	36
Lip Consonants	37
Point and Teeth Consonants	41
Front and Back Consonants	52
Throat Consonants	59
The Letters of the Alphabet, and their Phonetic Values in German	62
German Accent, and Other Peculiarities of German Pronunciation	98
Mode of Articulation	98
Laws of Sound	99
Stress and Emphasis	101
Tone (Pitch)	112
Specimens	115

LIST OF SYMBOLS USED IN PHONETIC SOUND NOTATION.

a = short of a:.
a: = (nearly) *a* in f*a*th*e*r.
ã = *an* in Fr. *an*.
aĭ = *ei* in G. b*ei*.
aŭ = *au* in G. B*au*.
b = *b* in *b*e.
ç = *ch* in G. i*ch*.
d = (nearly) *d* in *d*o.
e: = *ee* in G. S*ee*.
ɛ = (nearly) *e* in *le*t.
ɛ: = long of ɛ.
ɛ̃ = *in* in Fr. v*in*.
ə = *e* in G. all*e*.
f = *f* in *f*ee.
g = *g* in *g*o.
ɡ = occasional *g* in G. Ta*g*e.
h = (nearly) *h* in *h*e.
i: = *i* in G. m*i*r.
ɪ = *i* in *i*t.
j = (nearly) *y* in *y*es.
k = *k* in *k*ind.
l = *l* in *l*ow.
m = *m* in *m*e.
n = *n* in *n*o.
ŋ = *ng* in ri*ng*.

o: = *o* in G. s*o*.
ɔ = *o* in G. *o*b.
ɔ̃ = *on* in Fr. b*on*.
ɔy = *eu* in G. H*eu*.
ө: = *ö* in G. sch*ö*n.
œ or ɵ = *ö* in G. H*ö*lle.
œ̃ or ɵ̃ = *un* in Fr. *un*.
p = *p* in *p*ut.
r = trilled *r*.
s = *s* in *s*ee.
ʃ = *sh* in *sh*y.
t = *t* in *t*wo.
u: = *u* in G. d*u*.
ʊ = *u* in p*u*t.
v = *v* in *v*ie.
x = *ch* in G. a*ch*.
y: = *ü* in G. f*ü*r.
ʏ = *ü* in G. H*ü*tte.
z = *z* in *z*eal.
ʒ = *s* in plea*s*ure.
ʔ = throat stop (very slight cough).
ʹ = stress (precedes stressed syllable).
: = length.
~ = French nasality.

THE BEST GERMAN.

When Luther began to write, there was no generally acknowledged, truly national German language. Low German was used in conversation and literature throughout the North German plain, and High German in the mountainous regions of the South. Every province, and as far as the spoken language was concerned, every town or village, presented its own variety of idiom and pronunciation. But High German had long been in the ascendant, and many Low Germans were able to read and understand, if not to speak and write it. Luther wished to be read and understood all over Germany. To arrive at a "common German speech," as he himself remarks, he had only to be guided by the practice of the "Saxon Chancery," and indeed of "all the princes and kings in Germany," viz., to employ a High German freed as much as possible from all local and dialectal influences.[1]

---

[1] Bearing in mind that, according to Grimm's Law, *Sharp Mutes, Aspirates* (Spirants, etc.), and *Flat Mutes* in Low German (of which English will be even a better repre-

During the latter half of the sixteenth, and the first half of the seventeenth century, "Upper Saxon" (*Obersächsisch*), as his language used to be called, gradually absorbed the Low German literary dialects of the protestant northern half of the country; and by about the year 1700 Modern High German had not only firmly established itself as the common language of religion, of education, and of public business, but was also, in North German society, considered a more refined medium of intercourse than the Low German vernaculars. Yet even in our own times *Plattdeutsch* is far from being extinct as a colloquial language, and has been successfully used

---

sentative than the present Low German of Germany) ought to appear as *Aspirates* (Spirants, etc.), *Flat Mutes*, and *Sharp Mutes* respectively in High German, it will be easy to see from the following examples that Modern High German, though indeed clearly High German, does not carry the High German sound-shifting so far as some of the old Upper German dialects did, but distinctly betrays its Midland origin by taking an intermediate phonetic position.

{English:— {*pipe*   {*over*   {*bid*
{Low German:— {*Pipe*   {*awer*   {*bidden*
 High German:— *Pfeife*   *über*   *bitten*
{English:— {*town, sweet*   brother   {*daughter*
{Low German:—{*Tun, sôt*   {Bro*d*er {*Dochter*
 High German:— *Z*aun(*z* = ts), sû*fs* {Bru*d*er *T*ochter
  {English:—   {*cook*   {*goose*
  {Low German:— {*kaken*   {*G*os
   High German:— {*kochen*   {*G*ans

for literary purposes by such authors as Fritz Reuter and Klaus Groth.

In Middle and South Germany, the language of Luther was universally recognized as standard only after the year 1750; and a great number of spoken High German dialects are still flourishing by the side of the more or less closely allied language of literature.

It is only natural that, whenever Modern High German, the common language of the country, is employed orally, all the local peculiarities of dialectal utterance should be faithfully reflected in its pronunciation, in so far as they are not clearly interdicted by the spelling. As a matter of fact, it requires but little practice to distinguish, not only a North German from a South German, but a Hanoverian from a Westphalian, or a Bavarian from a Suabian, by hearing them read a single sentence from a book or newspaper.

Now, should the Germans themselves prefer this state of things to continue, every one, to use a popular phrase, talking *wie ihm der Schnabel gewachsen ist,* they are, of course, at liberty to do so. But this will not do for a foreigner who wants to acquire the language, and who certainly has a right to inquire where "the best German" is spoken.

English students of German, and English people in general, have put this question over and over again to the Germans they had nearest at hand, viz., the Hanoverians, and, naturally enough, they have just as many times been told that the best German is spoken in Hanover. What could they do but believe it? Yet it is a fact worth knowing that in Germany this belief is held only by the Hanoverians themselves.

Why indeed should any German think any other of the provincial pronunciations superior to his own? The *best* German, no doubt, ought to be better than any of them. In other words, we must have a spoken language which, like the written language of Luther, shall be superior to all dialects. We want something analogous to his "Saxon Chancery."

This we find in the language used on the German Stage, in which, although the same tendency to provincialism has always existed as in private life, the process of softening down and assimilating the different local modes of pronunciation has naturally been far more rapid. An actor whose Saxon pronunciation might appear quite the proper thing to an exclusively native public (which, of course, he would not have) at Dresden, would shock his hearers by speaking his part with the same pronunciation in Berlin or Vienna. Besides, any audience would be struck with the ludicrousness of a performance, say of Goethe's *Iphigenie,* with an Iphigenia from Pomerania, an Orestes from Friesland, a Pylades from the Tyrol, and so on. — On the stage, then, we

have the best German in practical use. There
are certainly even there moot points, which admit
of, and even demand, philological interposition;
but as far as it is settled, the language of the
theatre must be taken as the standard of German
pronunciation.

Now, if in the contest about the language of
literature the South has gained the victory over
the North, it is gratifying to see that with regard
to pronunciation the converse has taken place, the
Northern practice of distinguishing "voiceless" and
"voiced," instead of the Southern "hard" and "soft"
consonants, having been unanimously adopted on
the stage. Thus, as *lingua toscana in bocca romana* is considered the model spoken Italian, the
standard "common German speech" may be described as "High German word-forms pronounced
with Low German speech-sounds."

The High German word-forms being pretty
well fixed in the written language, whereas the
Low German speech-sounds have as yet found but
very little opportunity of making themselves palpable to the Southern population, German pronunciation, as a matter of course, will on the whole
be less removed from the standard in the North
than in the South of the country.

So far Hanoverian German is no doubt better
than that e. g. of Munich or Stuttgart. Yet it is
by no means free either from Low German misinterpretations of the High German spelling in

which the written language is set down, or from other strongly marked provincialisms.[1] A Hanoverian who should carefully avoid everything that is peculiarly Hanoverian in his speech, would be as good a model as any other.

Speaking generally, I would call him the best speaker who most effectually baffles all efforts to discover from what town or district he comes.

---

[1] The most noteworthy points are the following (for phonetic notations compare List of Symbols, page VIII): — 1. Initial Low German [sp-], [st-], instead of [ʃp-], [ʃt-], for *sp-*, *st-*, as in *spitz, stehen*. — 2. Inconsistent use of [g] for medial *-g-*, and of [ç] or [x] for final *-g*, as in *Siege, Sieg; Tage, Tag*. — 3. Shortening the radical vowel in monosyllables like *Bad, Lob*, etc. — 4. Mispronunciation of *a* as [æ:] instead of [a:], as in *Vater*. — 5. Mispronunciation of *ei*, or *ai*, and *au*, as [aï̯ë] and [aă̈], both almost sounding like [a:], instead of [aɪ̯], [aŭ], e. g. in *mein, Haus*. — 6. Use of [g] instead of [r] for *r*, as in *er, waren*, etc. — 7. Slurring over the vowel [ə] in the unaccented terminations *-em, -en*, at the same time allowing the [n-]sound to assimilate with the preceding consonant, e. g. *lieben* [li:bm] instead of [li:bən], etc.

GERMAN SOUNDS,
AND HOW THEY ARE REPRESENTED IN SPELLING.

1. VOWELS.

VOWELS, in German, as in English and other languages, are voice-sounds, consisting of a series of explosive puffs of air, from the glottis, acting on some definite configuration of the superglottal passages (mouth, throat, etc.). Vowel differentiation mainly depends, 1. on the position of the tongue, 2. on the shape of the lip aperture.

In the following diagram, the dotted line represents the roof of the mouth, the top line of the triangle connecting the centre of the hard palate with the centre of the soft palate. The positions of the letters [i], [u], etc. mark the positions of the articulating part of the tongue when pronouncing the vowel-sounds indicated by those letters in our table of phonetic sound-notation and presently to be described. Small parentheses in the diagram denote lip-rounding; a colon, length.

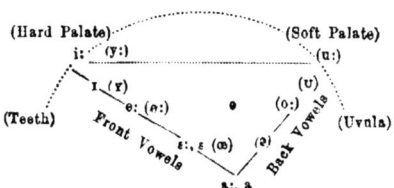

FRONT VOWELS.

HIGH-FRONT-NARROW VOWEL:[1] long, [i:]; shortened, [i]. (See table of phonetic sound-notation, p. VIII.) — If the tongue be raised as high and as close to the middle of the hard palate as is possible without causing friction, the vowel-sound produced will be the high-front-narrow vowel, or "close *i*" = [i].

Broadly speaking, English *i* in *machine*, or *e* in *he*, may be given as an instance of long close [i] = [i:]. In the London and South of England pronunciation it is generally, however, rather a diphthong, beginning with a somewhat more "open" *i*-sound, and only finishing with the close [i] in question, or even with the consonant [j], *he* thus being = [hɪːɪ], [hɪːj], not [hi:].

In French, all *i*'s, irrespectively of quantity, have this close sound.

In German, close [i] appears as a simple long vowel, and is spelt in the following ways: —

1. *i;* e. g. *mir* [miːr], me, to me.
2. *ie;* e. g. *sie* [ziː], she.
3. *ih;* e. g. *ihn* [ʔiːn], him.
4. *ieh;* e. g. *Vieh* [fiː], cattle.
5. *y*, in a few proper names; e. g. *Schwyz* [ʃviːts].[2]

---

[1] Adopting the terminology of Mr. A. M. Bell, which I find it possible to use, although I can only partly accept his analysis of vowel-articulation.

[2] So also unaccented final *y* in words borrowed from the English; e. g. *Sherry* [ʃɛriː], sherry.

6. *ee*, in a few words from the English; e. g. *Spleen* [spli:n], or [ʃpli:n], spleen.

If this sound occurs in "open" unaccented syllables,[1] it is more or less shortened, without, however, losing its close quality; e. g. *Militär* [mili'tɛ:r], military, army; *die gute* [di gu:tə], the good (fem. sing.). In very slow and distinct enunciation, secondary stress may preserve the full length of the vowel; e. g. [mi:li'tɛ:r], [di: gu:tə]. It could, indeed, hardly be called incorrect to retain [i:] everywhere, but it would certainly sound rather pedantic in conversation or informal reading. When final, [i:] retains its full length, e. g. *Alibi* [ˀa:libi:], alibi; *Pauli* [pau̯li:], of St. Paul (also a surname); as also when a simple word whose principal accent falls upon that sound is used as part of a compound, so that the principal accent becomes a secondary one; e. g. *Liebe* [li:bə], love; *Vorliebe* [fo:rli:bə], predilection.

₊ 1. Take care not to make German [i:] a diphthong, as *e*, *ee*, etc. in English; *nie* = [ni:], not [nɪ:ɪ], [nɪ:j], as English *knee*.

2. Avoid lowering the sound before final *r*, which in careful pronunciation is not an indistinct vocal murmur, [ə], as in English, but trilled [r]; *mir* thus being differently pronounced

---

[1] Compare the following chapter, on Letters and their Values.

from English *mere*, which may be [mɪːə], with open [ɪː], and is pronounced [mɪːr], [miːr] only by provincials.

3. Do not let [iː] be shortened by the influence of a following "sharp" or breath consonant, as is done in English, *fee* being [fiːj], and *feel* [fiːjl], but *feet* rather [fɪjt]. In German, the [iː] in *Gebiet* [gəbiːt], territory, is quite as long as the [iː] in *Vieh* [fiː], or in *viel* [fiːl], much.

4. Where [iː] in German is shortened, on account of not bearing the accent, do not substitute open *i* = [ɪ], or especially [ə], for it, but simply reduce it in quantity; e. g. *direkt* [diˈrɛkt], not [dɪrɛkt], with open [ɪ], or [dəˈrɛkt], as *direct* is occasionally pronounced in English.

HIGH-FRONT-NARROW-ROUND VOWEL: long, [yː]; shortened, [y]. — Pronounce the preceding vowel, [iː], at the same time rounding the lips, rather more than is the habit in pronouncing English *oo*, almost as in whistling, and the result will be the high-front-narrow-round vowel, or "close *ü*" = [yː].

This sound does not occur in English speech.

In French, all *u*'s are pronounced "close." — Welsh *u* in *du*, black, or *y* in *tŷ*, house, is not the same sound, but a "mixed" instead of a "round" vowel, i. e. articulated with a tongue-position intermediate between those for [i] and [u].

Its acoustic effect also is only similar to, not identical with, that of [y:].

In German, [y] is, like [i], used as a long vowel only, and represented in spelling by: —

1. *ü;* e. g. *für* [fy:r], for.

2. *üh;*[1] e. g. *kühn* [ky:n], bold.

3. *y,* in originally Greek words; e. g. *Asyl* [ʔa'zy:l], asylum, refuge.

4. *u,* sometimes followed by mute *e,* in words borrowed from the French; e. g. *Aperçu* [ʔapɛr'sy:], sketch, summary; *Revue* [rə'vy:], review.

This sound hardly occurs in unaccented open syllables, unless in words from the Greek or French. It is then shortened, like [i:]; e. g. *Tyrann* [ty'ran], tyrant; *Bureau* [by'ro:], office.

As to the pronunciation of *y,* many speakers treat this letter as if it were *i.* As, however, persons acquainted with Greek generally give it the same sound which the Greek letter *v* has in the German school pronunciation of Greek, viz. [y:], "good usage" certainly is in favour of the latter sound. Still, in words in common use, such as *Cylinder,* cylinder, but also meaning a tall hat, or a lamp chimney, the *y,* especially when unaccented, is almost universally pronounced [i:], [i]; e. g. [tsi'lɪndər]. Compare the mo-

---

[1] If the word-stem contains a *t,* the *h* is (in proper names) written after the *t,* e. g. *Thüringen,* Thuringia. Similary with other vowels.

dern spellings, *Gips*, gypsum; *Silbe*, syllable; *Kristall*, crystal. The above remarks equally apply to short open y = [Y].

In the Middle and South of Germany, the lip-rounding is often neglected in pronouncing [y:], and [y:] is thus converted into [i:]. This pronunciation is provincial. In poetry indeed *ü*, etc. is frequently made to rhyme with *i*, etc., but in correct pronunciation each retains its proper sound, and rhymes such as *grüfsen : fliefsen*, i. e. [gry:sən] : [fli:sən], although quite allowable, are imperfect rhymes. The same may be said with regard to short open [Y] and short open [I].

*** 1 Do not confound [y:] with English [ju:], or rather [ju:w], as pronounced in *muse*, *new*, etc. — [y:] is a simple sound, in which the tongue-position of [i:] and the lip-rounding of [u:] take place simultaneously.

2. The [y:]-sound must not be lowered before *r* [r]; e. g. in *für*.

3. It must not be shortened before breath consonants; e. g. in *süfs*.

HIGH-FRONT-WIDE VOWEL, [I]. — By slightly lowering and retracting the front of the tongue from the [i]-position, we arrive at the position for the high-front-wide vowel, or open *i* = [I].

An open *i*-sound is used in English for "short *i*," as in *bit*.

The German [I], which is also and exclusively short, is perhaps, in careful pronunciation, a shade less open than the common English "short *i*," but practice varies, and the difference may be disregarded. In spelling, German [ɪ] appears as: —

1. *i;* e. g. *mit* [mɪt], with.
2. *ie,* in a few words; e. g. *vierzehn* [fɪrtseːn], fourteen.
3. *y,* in some proper names and foreign words; e. g. *Hyrtl* [hɪrtəl] (proper name).

** 1. This sound is to be pronounced distinctly even in unaccented syllables; e. g. *Königin,* queen, must not be confused in pronunciation with *Königen,* (to) kings, the former being [køːnɪg/ɟɪn],[1] the latter [køːnɪg/ɟən].

2. Final *r* [r] must have no influence on [ɪ]; *Hirt* [hɪrt] has an [ɪ-]sound just as distinct as the one in *mit* [mɪt]. Avoid therefore any approach to [həːt], as English *hurt* (compare *dirt*) is pronounced.

HIGH-FRONT-WIDE-ROUND VOWEL, [ʏ]. — If the lips are rounded in pronouncing [ɪ], the sound is changed to the high-front-wide-round vowel, or open *ü* = [ʏ].

This also is not an English sound.

In German, [ʏ] is the short correspondent of [yː], as [ɪ] is of [iː]. It is spelt: —

1. *ü;* e. g. *Hütte* [hʏtə], hut.

---

[1] [g/j] = either [g], or [j].

2. *y,* in words originally Greek; e. g. *Myrte* [mʏrtə], myrtle.

3. *u,* in some loan-words from the French; e. g. *Budget* [bʏ'dʒeː], budget.

See the remarks on [yː], page 11.

⁎ The sound remains the same when followed by *r* [r].

MID-FRONT-NARROW VOWEL: long, [eː]; shortened, [e]. — On the articulating part of the tongue reaching about one third of the way from the position for [i] to the position for [a], the mouth cavity will serve as a resonance chamber for the mid-front-narrow vowel, or close *e* = [e].

This sound is not used in English, except, by some speakers, as the first element of the diphthong [eːɪ], for the "long *a*" in *pale*, etc., where others employ a more open [ɛ]-sound, making the diphthong = [ɛːɪ]. Scotch *ay* in *day*.

In French, *é fermé,* often written *é,* is the sound in question.

In German, long [e], i. e. [eː], is the sound given to "long *e,*" spelt: —

1. *e;* e. g. *schwer* [ʃveːr], heavy, difficult.
2. *ee;* e. g. *Beet* [beːt], flower-bed.
3. *eh;* e. g. *Reh* [reː], roe.
4. *ẹ́,* in words from the French, and sometimes in German proper names; e. g. *Carré,* now spelt *Karree,* [ka'reː], square, squadron.

In unaccented open syllables, except those

where [ə] is employed (see page 30), [eː] is shortened, but not changed to open [ɛ]; e. g. *Sekretär* [zekre′tɛːr], secretary. Final [eː], occurring in names originally Greek, etc., as in *Athene* [ʔa′teːneː], is again excepted. Likewise [eː] originally accented, when occurring in a portion of a compound not bearing the principal stress, still retains its length; e. g. *geben* [ɡeːbən], give; *ausgeben* [ʔaŭsɡeːbən], spend.

In a large part of Germany, long *e, ee,* or *eh,* is not always pronounced as [eː], but in certain words more or less open, = [ɛː]. These distinctions are, as a rule, accounted for by etymology; usage, however, is greatly at variance in the different localities, some districts retaining more of the older open sounds, others less. The modern tendency, which already prevails in some provinces, as also in Berlin, is certainly in favour of a uniform [eː], and this is the only pronunciation which can be recommended.

English students of German not trained in phonetics generally fail to perceive the difference between [eː] and [ɛː], which, however, is quite distinct to continental ears, and must not be disregarded.

₊ 1. Do not think you can substitute English "long *a,*" i. e. [eːɪ], or [ɛːɪ], for German [eː]. The finishing [ɪ]-sound must be carefully avoided. Compare German *Reh* [reː] with English *ray* [reːɪ] or [rɛːɪ].

2. The finishing [ɪ]-sound is omitted also in English before final *r* [ə], but then the *e*-sound itself is never [e:], but opener, [ɛ:], if not [æ:], the long of *a* in *cat; fare* thus being pronounced [fɛ:ə], or [fæ:ə]; *ere* [ɛ:ə], or [æ:ə], etc. Particular care must therefore be taken not to lower [e:] before *r* [r] in pronouncing German.

3. Allow the [e:] to retain its full length before breath consonants. There is no such difference in quantity between the vowel in *fehl,* amiss, [fe:l], and that in *gehst,* goest, [ge:st], as there is between the [e:ɪ] in *fail* [fe:ɪl], and the [eɪ] in *graced* [greɪst].

MID-FRONT-NARROW-ROUND-VOWEL: long, [ø:]; shortened, [ø]. — Round the preceding vowel, [e:], to get the mid-front-narrow-round vowel, or close *ö* = [ø:].

This again is not an English vowel. The nearest approximation to it in English is the vowel-sound in *her, bird, surd,* etc., as pronounced by many speakers. But this is at best a "mixed" instead of a "front-round" vowel, the middle instead of the front of the tongue being raised, without the "rounding" of the lips essential to German [ø:].

[ø] is the French *eu fermé*, as in *Meuse* (long), *Europe* (short).

In German, long *ö* is pronounced [ø:]. It is written: —

GERMAN SOUNDS.

1. *ö*, in a few originally foreign words followed by mute *e;* e. g. *schön* [ʃøːn], beautiful; *Diarrhöe* [diaˈrøː], diarrhœa.

2. *öh;* e. g. *Höhle* [høːlə], cave.

3. *eu*, sometimes followed by mute *e*, in words from the French: e. g. *adieu* [ʔadıˈøː], [ʔaˈdjøː], adieu, good bye; *Queue* [køː], cue.

4. *oeu,* also in French words (French spelling *œu*); e. g. *Coeur* [køːr], hearts (in cards).

It occurs in unaccented syllables in loanwords only. It is shortened in the same way as [iː], [yː], etc.; e. g. *Böotien* [bøˈoːtsi̯ən]. Bœotia.

In the provincial pronunciations of Middle and South Germany, [øː] is replaced by [eː], its unrounded correspondent, as [yː] is by [iː]. In correct usage, these sounds are always distinguished, even when they are made to rhyme in poetry; as *Höhle: Seele,* soul; i. e. [høːlə] : [zeːlə]. The same remarks hold good with regard to short open [œ] and the corresponding unrounded sound [ɛ].

*** 1. Keep the [øː] distinct from [yː], and do not confuse it with English [əː], as in *her, bird, surd,* etc.

2. See that the [øː] is not influenced by final *r* [r] following it. The vowel in *hört* [høˑrt], hears, etc., must be identical with the one in *Höhle* [høːlə]. This also applies to *eur* (*oeur*) in words originally French, where open [œː] is

the French sound; e. g. *Redakteur* [redak'tø:r], editor.

MID-FRONT-WIDE VOWEL, [ɛ]. — If the tongue is further lowered and drawn back in the direction of the line connecting the positions for [i] and [a], so that the position of the highest part of the tongue is at the centre, or not further backwards than the end of the central third of this line, the sound produced will be a mid-front-wide vowel, or a more or less "open *e*" = [ɛ].

An open *e*-sound, = [ɛ], is used in English for *e* in *bet* (short), whilst *a* in *care*, or *e* in *ere* (long), is lower (low-front-narrow).

Both [ɛː] and [ɛ] are employed in German.

Long "open *e*" = [ɛː], is the sound given to: —
1. *ä*; e. g. *säen* [zɛːən], sow.
2. *äh*; e. g. *mähen* [mɛːən], mow.
3. *ai*, in words originally French; e. g. *Palais* [pa'lɛː], castle.
4. *e*, before *r* [r], also in French words; e. g. *Dessert* [dɛ'sɛːr], dessert.

In unaccented open syllables, where [ɛː] hardly occurs in genuine German words, the sound is reduced in quantity, as other long vowels are; e. g. *plaidieren* [plɛ'diːrən], to plead.

There is a tendency to pronounce [eː] for [ɛː], in different parts of the country, also in Berlin; but this must still be considered as dialectal.

GERMAN SOUNDS.

*** Give all German [ɛ:]s, whether followed by r [r] or not, the vowel-sound of e in bet lengthened.

Short open e = [ɛ], is used for: —
1. e; e. g. fest [fɛst], fast, firm.
2. ä; e. g. Hände [hɛndə], hands (plur.).

There is no difference between "short e" and "short ä" in correct German pronunciation, although an artificial distinction is sometimes attempted by schoolmasters and others who are misled by the spelling and the analogy of "long e" and "long ä." In fact, the ä (for the short vowel) is only a comparatively modern spelling, based on etymological grounds, but by no means consistently carried out. In Middle High German, hende was written for Hände, and the old spelling is retained in the modern behende, "nimble," which is formed from the same stem. — Geld: fällt, and the like, form perfect rhymes — [gɛlt] : fɛlt], etc.

*** 1. Pronounce "short e" and "short ä" both as "short e" in Northern English = [ɛ], and do not think ä ought to be made like "short a" in fat, etc. — Gäste [gɛstə], guests, has the same vowel as English guests, etc.

2. Do not let [ɛ] in any way be influenced by final r [r] following it. Herr, the German for Mr., sir, may be pronounced [həː], as English her, in an English context, but this is by no means the German pronunciation of Herr; it is

[hɛr], with distinct short [ɛ] and the usual final [r]. So *Herz*, heart = [hɛrts], *Erbe*, heir = [ʔɛrbə], etc. The substitution of [əː] as in *her*, *bird*, etc., for [ɛr] and [ɪr] being one of the mistakes to which English speakers of German are most liable and to which they adhere most pertinaciously, particular care ought to be taken to avoid it.

Mid-front-wide-round vowel, [œ].[1] This is the rounded form of [ɛ].

In English it does not occur, the "mixed" [əː] used for the vowel in *her* being only similar to it, and, indeed, more similar to this open [œ]-sound than to the close [øː]. See remarks on [øː], page 16.

In German, [œ] is only used as a short vowel, and is always spelled:

ö; e. g. *Gespött* [gəʃpœt], mockery.

As to dialectal South German pronunciation and use in rhyme, compare [øː], page 17.

*** 1. Do not substitute [əː] as in *her*, etc. for German [œ], which above all must be pronounced short.

2. If followed by final *r* [r], [œ] must remain the same in quality and quantity as in other cases.

---

[1] Another phonetic symbol is [ɵ].

BACK VOWELS.

LOW-BACK-(WIDE) VOWEL, [a]. — A vowel-sound produced with the tongue in a position twice as far from the centre of the hard palate as from that of the soft, will be the low-back-(wide) vowel, [a], which, in acoustic effect, is equally remote from [i] and [u], or from [e] and [o], etc.

This is the sound used for the *a* in *father* by South of England speakers, the Northern pronunciation verging towards the *a* in *all*.

French *a* in *rare* is almost a front vowel; *a* in *pas* is practically the unrounded form of English *a* in *all*, though certainly not sufficient to identify it with the latter sound, as is done by some English speakers of French.

The *a* in *all* used to be be called the "German *a*" by older English grammarians, in opposition to the *a* in *father,* named the "Italian *a*." In point of fact, there is no such sound as this so-called German *a* in received German pronunciation, all German *a*'s, whether long or short, being pronounced as Italian *a*'s, i. e. as "pure" [a:], when long, and [a], when short.

The long sound, in German spelling, has the following symbols: —

1. *a;* e. g. *da* [da:], there.
2. *aa;* e. g. *Aal* [ʔa:l], eel.
3. *ah;* e. g. *nah* [na:], near.

4. *aw;* in the originally English word *Shawl* [ʃaːl], now spelt *Schal*, shawl.

5. *i,* as the second element of the originally French diphthong *oi,* in French pronounced [u̯aː], but in German [oaː]; e. g. *Boudoir* [budoˈaːr], boudoir.

In the South of Germany generally the sound is slightly lower, not quite so clear, but still does not approach the *a* in *all* so much as does the North English *a* in *father*. Not a few German dialects, as those of Thuringia, Saxony, Bavaria, and Austria, indeed, employ a broader "long *a,*" a sound similar to, or identical with, English *a* in *all*. But any such pronunciation, except where comical effects are intended, would be quite inadmissible on the stage. Hanoverian pronunciation sins in the opposite direction by giving the "long *a*" a mincing sound, like the one often heard for *a* in *path,* — *Vater,* father, almost being [fæːtər], etc.

Long [aː] in unaccented open syllables is shortened; e. g. *Kanone* [kaˈnoːnə], canon; but not when [aː] is final; e. g. *Anna* [ˀanaː], Ann, with fully long [aː]; nor is [aː] in secondarily accented parts of a compound thus reduced in quantity, if the [aː] has the primary accent when the word is used by itself; e. g. *Art* [ˀaːrt], kind, species; *Abart* [ˀapˀaːrt], variety.

⁎ 1. Let [aː] everywhere have the clear

sound of *a* in *far*, and avoid any approach either to *a* in *all* or to *a* in *care*.

2. If [aː] is followed by a vowel, either in the same word or in the beginning of the following word, take care not to insert an [r]-sound, as you may feel tempted to do from your English practice of saying e. g. [faː] for *far*, when not followed by a vowel, but [faːr], when followed by one; as, *is it far?* [ɪz ɪt faː?], but: *how far is it?* [haŭ faːr ɪz ɪt?]. Of course, if [aː] in German is followed by *r*, this must be pronounced as [r].

3. Do not convert unaccented [aː] into the indistinct vowel-sound [ə] used for unaccented back vowels in English, as in [pəpaː], for *papa*. In German the sound, although unaccented, retains its quality, e. g. *Papa* [pa'paː], and when final, also its quantity; *Anna* as stated above, being [ʔanaː], not [ʔana], and still less [ʔanə], which would be taken for *Anne* (a form of the name also in use).

Short [a], the same sound as [aː], only shortened, is spelt: —

1. *a*; e. g. *ab* [ʔap], off.
2. *i*, as the second element of the diphthong *oi* in some French loan-words; e. g. *Octroi* [ʔɔktro'a], excise.

As to dialectal varieties of [a], compare remarks on [aː].

*** 1. Do not confuse this sound with the

"short *a*" in *at, man*, which is not a pure *a*-sound, but intermediate between [a] and [ɛ]. Simply shorten the vowel in *far, father*.

2. Avoid lengthening [a] before *r* [r]; *hart*, *hard* = [hart], with short [a] followed by [r], not [haːət], [haːt], like English *hart*, or *heart*.

3. Keep the [a] distinct, also, when not accented. German [a] is never slurred over like unaccented *a* in *Arab, metal*, pronounced [ʔærəb], [mɛtəl], but retains its distinct sound; e. g. *niemand* [niːmant], nobody, not [niːmənt]; *Islam* [ʔɪslam], Islam, etc.

MID-BACK-WIDE-ROUND VOWEL, [ɔ]. — Raise the back of the tongue in the direction of the middle of the soft palate, so that at least one third or even one half of the distance between the tongue-height for [a] and that for [u] is reached, at the same time rounding the lips rather more than in pronouncing *o* in *note*. The sound produced will be the mid-back-wide-round vowel, or open *o* = [ɔ].

Many English speakers employ this sound as the first element of the diphthong [ɔŭ], pronounced for *o* in *note*, others making the *o*-element either closer or more open. Provincial *oo* in *door* may occasionally be the same sound (long), but it is closer in the North of England, and very much opener in the received Southern pronunciation, as is English "short *o*" in *not*.

French "open *o*," in *noce* (short), *nord* (long), is usually considered the same sound as the German [ɔ], but seems rather lower — though narrow — and more "advanced".

German [ɔ] is only used short, and always spelt: —

o; e. g. *ob* [ˀɔp], if, whether.

In some German dialects it becomes almost "close *o*" = [o], whilst others make it nearly as open as the English *o* in *not*.

* 1. Remember that English *o* in *not* is a much opener sound than German [ɔ], and therefore must not be used instead. It reminds a German ear of [a].

2. Let [ɔr], wherever it occurs, remain distinct short [ɔ] followed by [r]; *fort*, forth [fɔrt], not [fɔːət], [fɔːt], as English *fort*.

3. In unaccented syllables the sound does not become indistinct [ə], as *o* in *Jacob*, *abbot* in English, but retains its quality; e. g. *Jacob*, Jacob, James [jaːkɔp], not [jaːkəp], etc. This applies also to unaccented [ɔr], as in *Doktor* [dɔktɔr], doctor.

MID-BACK-NARROW-ROUND VOWEL, [o]. — If the articulating back of the tongue be raised still more towards the middle of the soft palate, so as to reach the end of the central third of the way from the [a]-position to the [u]-position, whilst the lips are rounded, we get the mid-back-narrow-round vowel, "close *o*" = [o].

A similar sound is sometimes used as the first element of the diphthongal sound given to *o* in *no* in English, but as a rule the English sound is more open. The same may be said of a provincial or antiquated close pronunciation of the *oo* in *door*. See remarks on [ɔ].

The French "close *o*" in *dos* is the sound meant.

Also "close *o*" in German is as a rule more distinctly rounded than English *o*-sounds. Accented, it occurs long only, bearing the same relation to short [ɔ], as [ø:] does to [œ]. The following spellings are in use for it: —

1. *o;* e. g. *so* [zo:], so.
2. *oo;* in very few words; e. g. *Boot* [bo:t], boat.
3. *oh;* e. g. *roh* [ro:], raw, rude.
4. *oe*, in Low German names; e. g. *Soest* [zo:st]; *Itzehoe* [ʔɪtsəho:].[1]
5. *oi*, also in Low German names; e. g. *Troisdorf* [tro:sdɔrf].[2]
6. *ow*, in Low German names, and in some English words; e. g. *Grabow* [ɡraːbo:]; *Bowle* [bo:lə], claret cup.

---

[1] Schiller makes it rhyme with *Musjeh*, as if pronounced [ʔɪtsəhøː].

[2] Now often pronounced [trɔÿsdɔrf], by railway officials, etc.

7. *au*, in words originally French; e. g. *Sauce*, now also spelt *Soſse*, [zoːsə], sauce.

8. *eau*, also a French spelling; e. g. *Plateau* [plaˈtoː], plateau.

9. *oa*, in some English loan-words; e. g. *Toast* [toːst], toast.

In some parts of Germany the "long *o*" is made too open. There is no long open *o* in received pronunciation.

If unaccented, [oː] is shortened, still retaining its close sound. Final [oː] always remains long. E. g. *Salomo* [zaːlomoː], Solomon.

*** 1. Do not make German [oː] a diphthong, as English *o* in *no*, which = [oːŭ]. *So* = [zoː], but English *so* = [soːŭ], or [sɔːŭ].

2. Do not shorten the sound before voiceless consonants, as [oːŭ] becomes [oŭ] in English *note*, whereas *node* has full [oːŭ]. Compare *Not* [noːt], need, and English *note* [noŭt].

3. Keep the sound close before final *r* [r]; *Ohr*, ear, being [ʔoːr], and not identical with English *or* [ɔːə], [ɔː].

HIGH-BACK-WIDE-ROUND VOWEL, [u]. — Let the back of the tongue be raised to the middle of the remaining distance between [o] and [u], and it will be in the position for the high-back-wide-round vowel, or "open *u*," [u], in pronouncing which the lips must at the same time be rounded.

English *u* in *put* and *oo* in *poor* are open *u*-sounds.

The German open [ʊ], which is only used short, is perhaps rather less open than English *u* in *put*, and more decidedly rounded. It is written: —

1. *u;* e. g. *Kunst* [kʊnst], art.
2. *ou*, in a few French words; e. g. *Ressource* [rɛ́sʊrsə], resource.

South German "short *u*" is almost a close *u*-sound.

⁎ 1. Let final *r* = [r] following [ʊ] have no influence on it, either in quality or in quantity. *Urne* [ˀʊrnə], urn, must have the same vowel-sound as *Kunst;* there is no approach whatever to the English pronunciation of *urn* [əːn].

2. Unaccented [ʊ] must not be made [ə], the indistinct vowel used for *u* in English *focus;* the German *Fokus* being pronounced [foːkʊs], with distinct [ʊ].

HIGH-BACK-NARROW-ROUND VOWEL, [u]. — Approach the back of the tongue as near to the middle of the soft palate as is possible without converting a vowel-sound uttered under these circumstances into a buzzed consonant, at the same time round the lips, to get the position for the high-back-narrow-round vowel, or "close *u*" = [u].

English "long *oo*" in *pool* is commonly considered as long [u] = [uː], but it is rather diphthongal [ʊːw], beginning with more open [ʊ] and only finishing with [ü], or even [w], just as *ee* in *feel* is rather [ɪːY], [ɪːj], than [iː].

In German, "long *u*" is always [uː], being the long correspondent of short [ʊ], as [iː] is of short [ɪ], etc. The German spellings for [uː] are: —

1. *u;* e. g. *du* [duː], thou.
2. *uh;* e. g. *Kuh* [kuː], cow.
3. *ou*, in some words from the French; e. g. *Tour* [tuːr], tour.

In unaccented syllables [uː] is shortened to [u], but not when it is final; e. g. *Mulatte* [muˈlatə], mulatto, but *Kakadu* [kakaduː], cockatoo. If the principal accent is lost on account of composition, the length of the [uː] remains unimpaired; e. g. *Zug* [tsuː^{k}/$_{x}$], pull, etc.; *Abzug* [ˈʔaptsuː^{k}/$_{x}$], deduction, etc.

*** 1. Try to make [uː] in German strictly monophthongal, distinguishing, e. g. *du* [duː], and English *do* [dʊːw].

2. Do not shorten this sound before voiceless consonants, as [ʊːw] is then reduced to [ʊw] in English; e. g. *goose* [gʊws].

3. Do not sink [uː] to [ʊː], still less to [oː] or [ɔː], before final [r], as English "long *oo*" is often pronounced when followed by *r* [ə], as in *poor* [pʊːə], [poːə], etc. Compare with this, German *Tour* = [tuːr].

MIXED VOWEL.

MID-MIXED VOWEL, [ə]. — By combining a relaxed [ɛ] front, and a still more relaxed [ɔ] back elevation of the tongue, the organs will be in the position for the mid-mixed vowel, generally called in German "unaccented *e*," [ə].

English *u* [ʌ] in *but* is often pronounced in a similar way, and still more frequently *ur* [əː] in *burn;* but the "indistinct vowel" [ə] in unaccented syllables, e. g. *a* in *drama*, *er* (mute *r*) in *better*, *o* in abbot, etc., comes perhaps nearest to the [ə-]sound in acoustic effect, although it is less distinctly articulated than German [ə], and especially wants the definite [ɛ]-element.

French *e* in *de* is not identical with the German "unaccented *e*," the French sound being rounded.

The only spelling used for German [ə] is: —

e; e. g. *Gebote* [gəboːtə], commandments, — except when *l* is written for *el* in proper names, e. g. *Vogl*, pronounced as *Vogel*, bird [foːqəl]. In similar word-endings, viz., — *el, em, en, er*, it is indeed not easy to distinguish [əl], [əm], [ən], [ər], from the simple sonsonants, [l], [m], [n], [r], in "syllabic" function, which are considered by many as the correct oral equivalents of the written syllables *el*, *em*, etc., and which are certainly very often substituted for [əl], [əm], etc. At all events, the [n-]sound ought to be kept distinct in the termination *en*, and such pronunciations as [le:bɪn], [lɛ:bm], or [le:m:], [lɛ:m:], with long [m], for *leben*, live, [ne:m:] for *nehmen*, take, [trɪŋkŋ] for *trinken*, drink, [zɪŋ:] for *singen*, sing, as well as [zɪn:] for *sinnen*, reflect, cannot pass for "correct" as long as [le:bən] or [le:bn], [ne:mən] or [ne:mn], [trɪŋkən] or [trɪŋkn], [zɪŋən] or [zɪŋn], and [zɪnən] appear perfectly natural and convenient forms to a vast number of speakers.[1]

"Unaccented *e*" is not pronounced uniformly throughout Germany. Instead of the [ə] described above, [ɛ], or almost [e], may be heard in South Germany, and in Silesia, whereas pronunciations verging towards [a] or [ɔ] are met with in the Northern half of the country.

*** 1. Do not use a distinct *e*-sound for final [ə], as also some English speakers of German are inclined to do.

2. Carefully avoid putting in an [r]-sound between final German [ə] — or rather English [ə], which you may have substituted for it — and a vowel-sound beginning the following word, as you say [bɛtə] for *better*, but [bɛtər ən bɛtə]

---

[1] Assimilations like [le:bm], [lɛ:bm], [le:m], [lɛ:m], etc., are by no means so general as is sometimes asserted, nor do they represent one of the characteristics of modern sound development, such forms as *lebm*, live, *gebm*, give, or *puechstam*, letter, occurring as early as 1542 and 1477.

for *better and better*, or [aɪdiːə] for *idea*, but perhaps [noːŭ aɪdiːər əv ɪt] for *no idea of it*, in English. To say [hatər ɪç] instead of [hatə ɪç] for *hatte ich*, or [zaːᵏ/ₓtər eːr],[1] instead of [zaːᵏ/ₓtə eːr], for *sagte er*, is altogether un-German.

DIPHTHONGS.

A diphthong is the combination of a full vowel with a semivowel, i. e. a vowel subordinated to the other by diminution of force, and often also reduction in quantity.

In German there are three diphthongs, all of them *decrescendo* diphthongs, i. e. with the full vowel preceding the semivowel. They are, [aɪ], [aŭ] and [ɔy̆] or [ɔɪ].

The first diphthong, [aɪ], is commonly identified with English *i* in *mine*, which, however, as a rule consists of a "mixed" vowel, perhaps more like *u* [ʌ] in *but* than like the short of *a* [aː] in *father*, followed by [i], or rather a "high-mixed" sound, the middle of the tongue being raised instead of the front.

The German [aɪ], the second element of

---

[1] Supposing the remaining sounds to be pronounced correctly. But I have heard [hætər ɪç], [sægtər ɔː], and the like.

which is often more or less "lowered," is represented in the received spelling in the following ways: —

1. *ei;* e. g. *Ei* [ʔaɪ̯], egg.
2. *ai,* in some German words, and in foreign words; e. g. *Mai* [maɪ̯], May; *Detail* [de'taɪ̯], detail.
3. *ey,* in proper names; e. g. *Meyer* [maɪ̯ər].
4. *ay,* likewise in proper names; e. g. *Bayern* [baɪ̯ərn], Bavaria.
5. *i,* in a few English loan-words; as *Strike,* now usually written *Streik* [ʃtraɪ̯k], strike.

The pronunciation [ɛɪ̯], [æɪ̯], for [aɪ̯], heard in parts of North as well as South Germany, is dialectal.

*** The first element of the English diphthong [aɪ̯] or [əɪ̯] = *i* in *mine* appears shorter even than usual when this diphthong is followed by a voiceless consonant, as in *ice* = [aɪ̯s], [äɪ̯s]. German [aɪ̯] must not be allowed to be thus affected, *Eis,* ice, being pronounced [ʔaɪ̯s], with the same [aɪ̯] as heard in *Ei* [ʔaɪ̯].

The second diphthong, [au̯], may without any great inexactness be taken as phonetically identical with English *ou* in *loud,* although here again the first element in the English diphthong seems usually to be rather a "mixed" vowel-sound, perhaps somewhat lower or opener than the first element of *i* [aɪ] in *mine*,[1] whilst in the second element the tongue-back will hardly reach the elevation required for [u].

In German as well, the second element is often "lowered," even by good speakers, but [aŭ] is to be considered the "correct" sound.

It is invariably spelt: —

au; e. g. *Au* [ʔaŭ], mead, meadow.

There is a provincial pronunciation [ɔŭ], for [aŭ], corresponding to the [ɛɪ], [æɪ] used instead of [aɪ].

⁎⁎ 1. Avoid substituting either a mixed vowel of the [ə]-type, as *u* in *but*, or any other sound, for the first element of [aŭ], but use the short of [a:], as pronounced in *father*.

2, Do not let the [a] of [aŭ] be shortened through the influence of a voiceless consonant following it, as may be the case in English, the [a] of [aŭ] in *out* [aŭt] being shorter than in *loud* [laŭd].

The third diphthong, [ɔy], [ɔɪ], is similar to English *oi* in *oil*, but the *o* in the latter is a more open vowel, and the second element is rather a mixed vowel, the same as the second element of *i* in *mine*.

In German, instead of [ɔẙ] or [ɔɪ], [ɔŏ] or

---

[1] The Cockney pronunciation approaches [æŭ], with [æ] = *a* in *hat*.

GERMAN SOUNDS.

[ɔœ̯] is frequently pronounced; see remarks on [aɪ̯]. There is another pronunciation, [œy̆], [œɪ̯], heard in the North-East and other parts of Germany, but [ɔy], [ɔɪ̯] is the more usual form. Other varieties of this third diphthong occur in provincial pronunciation; e. g. [ay̆], [æy̆].

The spellings used for this diphthong are:
1. *eu;* e. g. *Heu* [hɔy̆], hay.
2. *äu;* e. g. *gläubig* [glɔy̆bɪ⁽ᵏ⁾/ᵧ], believing.
3. *oi,* in originally Low German words; e. g. *Boi* [bɔy̆], buoy.

⁎ Take care not to make the [ɔ] of [ɔy̆] very open, nor to prolong it, as in English *oi* in *oil*. In the German [ɔy̆] the [ɔ] should be short and only moderately open.

NASAL VOWELS.

Any vowel may be made nasal, by lowering the uvula during its articulation and thus allowing the nose to serve as a resonance chamber in addition to the mouth cavity. Nasal vowels are not used in genuine German words, but occur in words borrowed from the French language. Although they are very generally replaced by a "pure" oral vowel followed by the nasal consonant [ŋ] = *ng* in *ring*,[1] especially in the North of Germany, careful speakers will retain

---

[1] The same is commonly done in English.

them. They are however all pronounced long, whatever may be their quantity in French.

The French spelling is always preserved; e. g. *Ballon* [ba'lɔ̃ː], balloon, *Chance* [ʃãːsə], chance, *Bassin* [ba'sɛ̃ː], basin, *Vingt-un* [vɛ̃ː'tœ̃ː], rather than [ba'lɔŋ], [ʃaŋsə], [ba'sɛŋ], [vɛŋ'tœŋ].

*** English speakers of German must be careful to give these nasal vowels their proper values, apart from the nasality, and especially not to confuse [ãː] and [ɔ̃ː], which are kept quite as distinct in German as they are in French.

2. CONSONANTS.

CONSONANTS are speech-sounds produced by either squeezing or stopping the outgoing breath in some part of the mouth or throat. Squeezed consonants are called "continuants;" stopped consonants, "stops," or "explodents."

A voice-sound (vocal murmur) may be combined with any consonant of either class. Thus we have to distinguish between voiceless (or "breath") stops or continuants, and voiced (or "voice") stops or continuants. Voiceless consonants are, as a rule, pronounced more forcibly than voiced ones; so the former are commonly called "sharp," and the latter, "flat."

Voiced consonants, except liquids and nasals, do not occur final in German pronunciation.

If, whilst assuming any "stop" articulation,

we allow the air to pass out through the nose, by lowering the uvula, we obtain the corresponding "nasal" consonant.

The following diagram, which should be compared with the one given on page 7, shows the places in which the various stops and friction channels are formed.

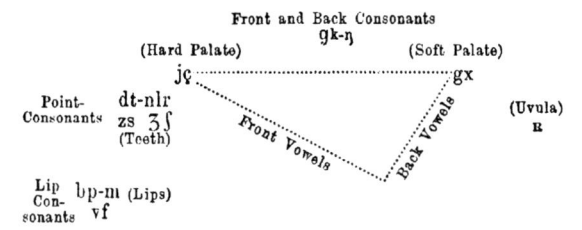

```
                    Front and Back Consonants
                           gk-ŋ
        (Hard Palate)              (Soft Palate)
              jç..............................gx
Point-     dt-nlr                                    (Uvula)
Consonants zs ʒʃ       Front Vowels   Back Vowels      ʀ
           (Teeth)

 Lip     bp-m (Lips)
 Con-
sonants   vf
```

LIP CONSONANTS.

LIP-STOP-BREATH, [p]. — This consonant is formed by closing and reopening[1] the lips.

It is the sound of English *p* in *pea*, *lip*.

The German [p] is the same, except in the combination [pf], when the [p]-stop is usually, because more conveniently, effected by pressing the lower lip against the upper teeth, the following continuant [f] having this lip-teeth articulation. Initial [p] preceding an accented vowel, or final [p] following one, is aspirated, i. e. pronounced with a forcible emission of breath,

---

[1] Sometimes closing or opening only, according to the position in which the [p] occurs.

almost as [p + h]; and this is often the case in English also.

German [p] is spelt: —

1. *p*, e. g. *Paar* [pa:r], pair.
2. *pp*, after short vowels; e. g. *Rappe* [rapə], black horse.
3. *b* final, i. e. followed by no other letter, or by consonants only, e. g. *ab* [ˀap], off.

In the Middle and South of Germany, [p] is as a rule used in conversation, etc., in the beginning of a certain number of words only, whilst in all other cases Middle and South German speakers substitute for [p] their flat but voiceless [b]-sound, = [b̥], mentioned in the following section; and similarly with other stops. In some parts of the country (e. g., the kingdom of Saxony) the confusion is still greater.

The confusion in the pronunciation of consonants made by many German speakers of English, and so amusingly illustrated in "Punch" and other comic papers, is explained partly by these dialectal peculiarities, and partly by the well established German sound-law, by no means a dialectal one, that *all final consonants, except liquids and nasals, are pronounced voiceless and sharp* (page 36).

LIP-STOP-VOICE, [b]. — Same as preceding sound, only pronounced voiced and flat.

English *b* in *be, rib*.

German [b], which, like other voiced consonants, does not occur at the end of a word, has only two spellings: —

1. *b*, e. g. *Bahn* [baːn], track, railway.

2. *bb*, in Low German and other loan-words; e. g. *Ebbe* [ʔɛbə], ebb.

The Middle and South German *b*, = [b̥], is voiceless, and might almost be described as a very weak [p]. This sound is also often used instead of [p], as has been remarked in the preceding section. For *b* medial, the lip-lip continuant alluded to on page 40, is generally heard in Middle and South Germany; e. g. *Liebe* [liːvə].

LIP-STOP-VOICE-NASAL, [m]. — English *m* in *me, am*.

German [m] is identical with the English,[1] only *when final after a short vowel, it is pronounced shorter than English* [m]. This remark applies to all German and English consonants; but only in the "liquid" sounds [m], [n], [ŋ], [r], [l] need the difference be particularly insisted upon.

German [m] is spelt: —

1. *m*, e. g. *mir* [miːr], (to) me.

---

[1] *mpf*, as in *Kampf*, fight, is often [mf] with lip-teeth [m].

2. *mm*, after short vowels; e. g. *Lamm* [lam], lamb.

* Pronounce [m] final abruptly after a short vowel, as in *Lamm*.

LIP - TEETH - CONTINUANT - BREATH, [f]. — In uttering this "labio-dental" sound the lower lip is pressed against the upper teeth. English *f* in *fee, if*.

The following spellings occur for [f]: —

1. *f*, e. g. *Fall* [fal], fall.
2. *ff*, after short vowels; e. g. *Schiff* [ʃɪf], ship.
3. *v*, e. g. *viel* [fi:l], much.
4. *ph*, mostly in words originally Greek; e. g. *Philosoph* [filo'zo:f], philosopher.
5. *pph*, in the Greek name *Sappho* [zafo:].

LIP - TEETH - CONTINUANT - VOICE, [v]. — Same sound, flat and voiced.

German [v] is like English *v* in *very*, but less distinctly buzzed. It is spelt: —

1. *w*, e. g. *wohl* [vo:l], well.
2. *v*, only in foreign words; e. g. *Vase* [va:zə], vase.
3. *u*, in the combination *qu*; e. g. *Qual* [kva:l], torture.
4. *wh*, in the English word *Whist* [vɪst], whist.

In Middle and part of South Germany the lip-teeth continuant [v] is replaced by a lip-lip continuant [υ], which indeed hardly deserves the name of continuant, as it is pronounced very rapidly, so that, as a rule, also its vocal quality is lost, or becomes indistinct (= v̯).

In the combinations *qu* and *schw*, that is to say after the sounds [k] and [ʃ], the lip-lip [v] is generally resorted to also by North German speakers, the sound, as a rule, becoming at the same time voiceless, on account of its close connection with the voiceless [k] or [ʃ] preceding it.

Also when voiced, both the North and the South German lip-lip continuant are quite distinct from the sound of English *w* in *we*, or *u* in *queen*, as neither are the lips rounded nor is the back of the tongue raised in their pronunciation.

*** 1. Buzz German [v] less strongly than English [v].

2. Do not confuse German *qu* in pronunciation with English *qu*, nor pronounce German *schw* as you would pronounce *shw* in English. Compare *Quell* [kvɛl], well, with English *quell* [kwɛl].

POINT AND TEETH CONSONANTS.

POINT-STOP-BREATH, [t]. — German [t] is pronounced by pressing for a moment either the tongue-point or else part of the tongue-blade (the upper surface of the tongue-front immediately behind the point) against the roots of the upper teeth. The former mode is used in the North, the latter in the South of the country.

In pronouncing English [t], the tongue point

is in a similar position to that of North German [t], but at the same time a portion of the hard palate appears to be covered by the tongue-blade. Thus English [t] approaches a front-stop consonant, or forward [k],[1] and has a decidedly "thicker" effect than German [t].

As to "aspirated" [t], see page 37, on [p].

For [t] we have the following spellings: —
1. *t,* e. g. *Tau* [taŭ], rope.
2. *tt,* after short vowels; e. g. *fett* [fɛt], fat.
3. *th,* e. g. *Thron* [troːn], throne.
4. *d* final, e. g. *Hand* [hant], hand.
5. *dt,* only rarely; e. g. *Stadt* [ʃtat], town.

South and Middle German practice generally replaces [t] by "voiceless [d]" = [d̥]. See following section and remarks on [p], page 37.

*** In pronouncing German [t], try to form the stoppage between the tongue-point and the teeth-roots only. It is almost a stopped [θ] = *th* in *thin*.

POINT-STOP-VOICE, [d]. — Same sound, flat and voiced.

German [d] is represented by: —
1. *d,* e. g. *du* [duː], thou.
2. *dd,* after short vowels, in Low German or foreign words; e. g. *Kladde* [kladə], waste-book.

---

[1] It is not always easy to keep English [t] and [k] distinct; *at least* will sound like *ac least, clay* like *tlay,* etc. No such difficulty is experienced in German.

As to South and Middle German "voiceless [d]" = [d], compare remark on [b], page 39.

POINT-STOP-VOICE-NASAL, [n]. — The mouth-closure is the same as in German [t] or [d]. See also remarks on [m], page 39.

German [n] appears in spelling as: —

1. *n*, e. g. *nie* [niː], never.

2. *nn*, after short vowels; e. g. *Mann* [man], man.

₊ Pronounce [n] final short after a short vowel as well as in other positions.

TEETH-CONTINUANT-BREATH (THIN), [s]. — In producing this sound, the breath is directed on to the teeth, by means of a narrow channel running in the longitudinal central line of the tongue-blade. The latter (in North German pronunciation a more forward part than in South German pronunciation) approaches the gums just behind the upper teeth, but the sound owes its sibilance to the friction which the breath undergoes in passing out between the upper and lower front teeth.

English [s] is very similar to North German [s], but probably rather "wider" in its tongue articulation.

German [s] is written: —

1. *s* (in Gothic — or "German" — characters ẞ; and ſ before consonants, except initial *sp* and *st*, where *s* = [ʃ]), e. g. *List* [lɪst], stratagem.

2. *ss* (represented by ſſ in Gothic caracters), after short vowels; e. g. *Kasse* [kasə], cash.

3. *ſs* (still frequently printed *ss;* Gothic equivalent, ß, not ſſ), e. g. *Fuſs* [fuːs], foot.

4. *c* and *ç*, in words from the French; e. g. *Annonce* [ʔaˈnɔ̃ːsə], advertisement, *Façon*, now *Fasson*, [faˈsɔ̃ː], shape.

Besides *ts, tts*, etc., the combination [ts] is also spelt in the following ways: —

1. *z*, e. g. *zu* [tsuː], to, too.

2. *tz*, after short vowels; e. g. *Satz* [zats], sentence.

3. *c*, before front vowels, in foreign words; e. g. *Cis* [tsɪs], C sharp.

4. *t*, before unaccented *i*, in foreign words; e. g. *Nation* [natsˈiˑoːn], nation.

5. *zz*, in some Italian words; e. g. *Skizze*, [skɪtsə], sketch.

For [ks], besides *ks, chs*, etc., we also have the spelling: —

x, e. g. *Axt* [ʔakst], axe.

In Middle and South Germany, [s] is pronounced less strongly than in the North, and in no way differs from the sound used for North German [z]. See the following section.

*** Bear in mind that, although the same letter as English *z*, German *z*, apart from a few loan-words, has quite another phonetic value, i. e. [ts], the [t] and the [s] closely connected, but both pronounced strongly and distinctly =

GERMAN SOUNDS.

[t] and [s]. To pronounce German *z* = [z], like English *z*, is utterly wrong; and the compromise tried by many English speakers of German, to make it = [dz], is not much better. Compare: — English *zeal* [ziːjl], German *Ziel* [tsiːl], aim.

TEETH-CONTINUANT-VOICE (THIN), [z]. — Same sound, flat and voiced.

English *z* in *zeal*, or *s* in *lose*.

In German it is spelt: —

1. *s* (always ſ when Gothic characters are used), only before vowels or liquids; e. g. *so* [zoː], so.

2. *z*, only in some foreign words: e. g. *Gaze* [gaːzə], gauze.

This voiced sound is generally recognized only in the North of Germany, and in a large part of it [sz] is heard for initial [z].

In the Middle and South both for this and the preceding sound, a rather flat [s]-sound is used indiscriminately, which might be defined as "voiceless [z]." Middle and South German poets, Goethe and Schiller not excepted, therefore do not object to rhymes such as *Größe : Getöse*. Between vowels, however, this [z] frequently becomes voiced, no matter whether it stands for the North German [z], or [s].

On the stage [s] and [ʐ] are kept distinct.

TEETH-CONTINUANT-BREATH (BROAD), [ʃ]. — The "broad" sibilant in German is formed by the breath escaping in a broad current between the upper and lower teeth-rows, whilst the lips are protruded, in order to increase the resonance of the hissing sound produced by the friction of the breath passing over the edges of the teeth.

English [ʃ], the sound of *sh* in *shy*, has a different articulation, the blade of the tongue being retracted and approached to the hard palate, thus forming a second friction channel in addition to the one supplied by the teeth; protrusion of the lips, on the other hand, is dispensed with.

For German [ʃ] the following spellings are used: —

1. *sch* (ſch in Gothic characters), e. g. *scharf* [ʃarf], sharp.

2. *s* initial before *p* or *t* (ſp, ſt in Gothic characters), e. g. *sprechen* [ʃprɛçən], speak, *stehen* [ʃteːən], stand.

3. *ch*, only in French words; e. g. *Chef* [ʃɛf], head, principal.

4. *c*, in Italian words, e. g. *Cello* [ʃɛloː], violoncello.

5. *sh*, in English words; e. g. *Shawl* [ʃaːl], shawl.

6. *x*, in *Don Quixote*, which is generally pronounced after the French fashion — [dɔ̃ːkiʃɔt].

GERMAN SOUNDS. 47

Besides *tsch*, [tʃ] is also spelt: —

ch, in foreign words; e. g. *Guttapercha* [gʊta'pɛrtʃaː], gutta percha.

In large districts of the originally Low German part of the country, and also in Hanover, initial *s* preceding *p* or *t*, as in *sprechen, stehen,* is pronounced [s], in accordance with the spelling.

This provincialism is to be explained in the following way.

In Middle High German, not only the present initial *sp* and *st* (corresponding to *sp* and *st* in the cognate English words, e. g. *sprechen* = *speak*, *stehen* = *stand*) but also the modern initial *schl, schm, schn,* and *schw* (corresponding to English *sl, sm, sn,* and *sw*, e. g. *schlagen* = *slay, Schmerz* = *smart, Schnee* = *snow, schwimmen* = *swim*) were spelled with *s*, the pronunciation everywhere being [s].

From explicit statements of grammarians writing in the first half of the sixteenth century, we know, however, that in all these cases, *sp* and *st* included, the *s* had in their time come to be pronounced the same as *sch*, and that *sch* instead of *s* was often, as now regularly, written before *l, m, n,* and *w*, but rarely before *p* and *t*, where the old habit of writing *s* prevailed in the end.[1]

---

[1] Probably on account of the frequent occurrence of medial and final *sp* and *st* in German, as well as of

When the Low Germans, in learning the literary High German, came across such spellings as *sprechen* and *stehen*, they pronounced the *sp* and *st* all the more readily [sp] and [st], as initial *sp* or *st* never had — and, in fact, never has, up to the present day — been pronounced otherwise in the corresponding Low German words, with which they had hitherto been, and continued to be, familiar.

Thus [sprɛçən] and [steːən] etc., for [ʃprɛçən] and [ʃteːən] clearly are hybridisms, which cannot be admitted in good pronunciation, and have deservedly been banished from the stage, *even in the town of Hanover itself*.

⁎ 1. Try to pronounce German [ʃ] without pointing the tip of the tongue towards the gums or the hard palate.

2. Remember that initial *sp* and *st* stand for *schp* and *scht*, and that to pronounce [s], instead of [ʃ], in these combinations, would be substituting a Low German and English for the correct High German sound.

TEETH-CONTINUANT-VOICE (BROAD), [ʒ]. — Same sound, flat and voiced.

English [ʒ] = *s* in *pleasure* differs from German [ʒ], as English [ʃ] does from German [ʃ].

---

initial *sp* and *st* in Latin. Moreover, *schpr*, *schtr* (the other combinations, *sl*, *sm*, etc., do not occur before *r*, or any other consonant) would have looked very ungainly.

This sound is not a genuine German sound, but has been borrowed from abroad, together with its spellings: —

1. *j*, mostly in French words; e. g. *Journal* [ʒʊr'naːl], journal.

2. *g*, and *ge*, in words originally French, Italian, etc.; e. g. *Logis* [lo'ʒiː], lodging, *Sergeant* [zɛr'ʒant], sergeant.

The combination [dʒ], which also does not occur in originally German words, is spelt in the same ways: —

1. *j*, in a few English words; e. g. *Jockey* [dʒɔkaɪ], jockey.

2. *g*, also in English loan-words; e. g. *Gentleman* [dʒɛntəlmən], gentleman.

The [d] is, however, often omitted, [dʒɔkaɪ], [dʒɛntəlmən] thus becoming [ʒɔkaɪ], [ʒɛntəlmən], etc.

In the Middle and South of Germany, the [ʒ]-sound is not recognised, and [ʒ], [dʒ] are pronounced as if spelled *sch*, *tsch*, only not so strongly as North German [ʃ], [tʃ], — voiceless, but flat. See remarks on [z], page 45.

POINT-CONTINUANT-VOICE (TRILLED), [r]. — German lingual [r] is formed by bringing the tongue-point loosely against the gums and causing it to vibrate by means of the outgoing breath. It is, as a rule, voiced, but occasionally it becomes partly voiceless when closely connected with breath-consonants.

English [r] (initial or medial) has a similar tongue-position, but is not trilled, or trilled very slightly, except in provincial (Scotch, Irish, etc.) pronunciation.

German [r] is represented by: —

1. *r*, e. g. *rauh* [raŭ], rough.

2. *rr*, after short vowels; e.g. *Narr* [nar], fool.

3. *rh*, and *rrh*, in words originally Greek; e. g. *Rhabarber* [ra'barbər], rhubarb; *Katarrh* [ka'tar], catarrh, cold.

Tongue-point [r] is still the only one admitted in artistic singing, and in the stage-language, apart from farcical comedies and the like. In general use it is, however, rapidly losing ground before the "uvular" or "guttural" [ʀ] (uvular trill), in England known as the "Northumbrian burr," which already prevails in large districts, both in North and South Germany, especially the larger towns.

This is to be regretted, as the guttural [ʀ] is certainly a less pleasing sound than the lingual [r], and if not distinctly trilled, is very apt to clash with the back-continuants [g] and [x], thus *Waren*, goods, sounding like *Wagen*, carriage, *wart*, (you) were, like *wagt*, ventures, etc.

Final *r* = [r], and *er* = [ər], are mostly weaker. They have, with a vast number of speakers, entirely lost their [r]-sound, and have become an open vowel, mostly some kind of [a]. Thus a native of Berlin will call himself, not a [bɛr'liːnər], but a [bɛa'liːna]; *hier*, here, is pronounced [hiːa], *sehr*, very, [zeːa]; *vor*, before, [foːa], *nur*, only, [nuːa]; *war*, was, [vaː] or [vaːə]; *Kinder*, children, [kɪnda], etc.; just as English *here* has become, at least in the South, [hiːə], *there*, [ðɛːə], *poor*, [pʊːə], *far*, [faːə] or [faː], *better*, [bɛtə], except when immediately followed by another word beginning with a vowel, when final *r* in English (not in German) recovers its [r]-sound.

But the final "vocal" *r* = [a], etc., is not yet considered as belonging to "correct" German pronunciation, and can, therefore, just as little be recommended to English speakers of German, as can the "guttural" *r* = [R].

₊ Pronounce *r (rr, rh, rrh)* wherever it occurs in German spelling, also when final, as tongue-point [r]; also avoid lengthening an accented short vowel preceding final *r* as in *hart*, hard, which is pronounced [hart], and not with long *a*, as e. g. in *zart*, tender, = [tsaːrt].

POINT-TEETH-CONTINUANT-VOICE (DIVIDED), [l]. — Whilst the tip of the tongue forms a centre stop against the gums, the breath is allowed to escape between the sides of the tongue and the teeth. The back of the tongue is not raised, as it is in pronouncing English [l], which by this receives a guttural character. Like [r], [l] is regularly voiced.

There are only two spellings for German [l]:

1. *l*, e. g. *lahm* [laːm], lame.

2. *ll*, after short vowels; e. g. *voll* [fɔl], full.

⁎ The back of the tongue must be kept down in pronouncing German [l], especially when final, to avoid gutturality.

FRONT AND BACK CONSONANTS.

BACK-STOP-BREATH, [k]. — This stop is formed, as in English, between the back of the tongue and a more or less forward part of the palate, according to the sound following or preceding the [k]-sound. In articulating German [k], however, a smaller portion of the palate is covered, and it is therefore less "thick" in its acoustic effect than the English sound. The spelling varies greatly: —

1. *k*, e. g. *kahl*, [kaːl], bald.

2. *ck*, after short vowels; e. g. *dick* [dɪk], thick.

3. *ch*, in a number of German words, when followed by *s* = [s]; e. g. *Achse* [ˀaksə], axle; also in many foreign words, names, etc., e. g. *Chor* [koːr], choir.

4. *q*, always followed by *u* = [v] (or [v], page 41); e. g. *Quelle* [kvɛlə], well, spring; in foreign words sometimes preceded by *c*, which is not pronounced separately; e. g. *Acquisition* [ˀakvizitsǐoːn], acquisition.

GERMAN SOUNDS.

5. *c*, in foreign words; e. g. *Cognac*, now spelt *Kognak*, [kɔnjak], cognac.

6. *cc*, also in foreign words; e. g. *Accord*, now *Akkord*, [ʔa'kɔrt], accord.

7. *g* final; (*a*) used alternatively with [ç], after front vowels, and after consonants; e. g. *Sieg* [ziːk] or [ziːç], victory, *Berg* [bɛrk] or [bɛrç], mountain, and with [x], after back consonants, e. g. *Tag* [taːk] or [taːx], day, *zog* [tsoːk] or [tsoːx], drew (sing.); (*b*) regularly, followed by *s*, in *flugs* [flʊks],[1] quickly, as also in a few foreign words, e. g. *Log* [lɔk], log.

8. *gg* final, in a few foreign words; e. g. *Brigg* [brɪk], brig.

BACK-STOP-VOICE, [ɡ]. — Same sound, flat and voiced.

English [ɡ], as pronounced in *go*, *beg*, differs from German [ɡ], as English [k] does from German [k].

The German spellings are: —

1. *g;* (*a*) medial,[2] used alternatively with [j], after front vowels, and after consonants, e. g. *Siege* [ziːɡə] or [ziːjə], victories, *Berge* [bɛrɡə] or [bɛrjə], mountains, and with [g], after

---

[1] Originally genitive case of *Flug*, flight, which was *vluc* = [flʊk] in Middle High German, but is now [fluːk/x].

[2] i. e., in the interior of the word, including inflections, but not suffixes, such as *-nis*, *-lich*, etc.

back vowels, e. g. *Tage* [taːgə] or [taːgə], days, *zogen* [tsoːgən] or [tsoːgən], drew (plur.); (*b*) initial, regularly; e. g. *gut* [guːt], good, also after prefixes, like *be-, ge-, ver-, zer-* etc., and in composition; e. g. *vergehen*, pass away, [fɛrˈgeːən], *abgehen*, go away, [ˀapgeːən], as *gehen*, go, [geːən]; or, in foreign words, in the beginning of the accented syllable, e. g. *regieren* [reˈgiːrən], reign, *Kongress* [kɔnˈgrɛs], congress.

2. *gg*, after short vowels, in Low German loan-words, etc.; e. g. *Flagge* [flagə], flag.

3. *gu*, in foreign words, e. g. *Guinee* [giˈneː], guinea.

In North German provincial pronunciations, the corresponding continuants, [j], [g], [ç], or [x] are used instead of initial [g]; e. g. [j] in Berlin *gut* [juːt], [x] in Westphalian *gut* [xuːt].

BACK-STOP-VOICE-NASAL, [ŋ]. — The mouth-closure is the same as for [k] or [g]. English *ng* in *singer*.

See remarks on [m], page 39.

This sound, which, as in English, does not occur at the beginning of a word, is represented by:

1. *ng*, e. g. *singen* [zɪŋən], sing, *lang* [laŋ], long.

2. *n*, before [k] or, in foreign words, [g]; e. g. *Dank* [daŋk], thanks, *Albalonga* [ˀalbaː-ˈlɔŋgaː] (name).

Final *ng*, as in *lang*, is pronounced [ŋk], instead of [ŋ] simply, in a great part of North

GERMAN SOUNDS. 55

Germany; [ŋg] instead of [ŋ] = medial *ng,* as in *singen,* is heard in Westphalia only. These provincialisms are gradually retreating before the simple [ŋ]. On the other hand, [ŋn] instead of [gn] in foreign words, such as *Agnes* [ʔagnɛs], [ʔaŋnɛs] (name), is still very frequent.

** [ŋ], which is only found after short vowels, must be pronounced abruptly.

FRONT-CONTINUANT-BREATH, [ç]. — This consonant, the so-called *"ich*-Laut," is formed between the front of the tongue and the middle of the hard palate, in the same place where the vowel [i] is articulated.

It is not a regular English consonant, but sometimes occurs as the initial sound of *hue, hew,* etc.

In German, we have the two spellings: —

1. *ch,* after front vowels, and after consonants; e. g. *ich* [ʔɪç], I, *solch* [zɔlç], such; also initial *ch* in many foreign words; e. g. *Charon* [çaːrɔn] (proper name).

2. *g* final, after front vowels, and after consonants (used alternatively with [k], see page 53); e. g. *Sieg* [ziːç], victory, *Berg* [bɛrç], mountain. The suffix *-ig,* as in *König,* king, is pronounced [ɪç] by many speakers who generally use [k] for *-g.*

In certain districts, this sound approaches [ʃ], especially English [ʃ], for which see page 46.

In good pronunciation, the two sounds are kept distinct. Instead of [ç], in the North-East the back continuant [x] is used before back vowels, as in *Charon*.

∗ 1. Take care to keep [ç] distinct as well from [ʃ] as from the back-continuant or "*ach*-Laut," [x], which is quite a different sound. Compare the diagram on page 37, and the remarks on [x], page 58.

2. Pronounce final *g* after front vowels, etc., either exactly the same as *k*, or exactly the same as *ch* in *ich*, i. e. as a sharp voiceless consonant, and not as a voiced, or half-voiced one, as Englishmen are inclined to do. Final [ɡ], or [j], or [g], although not unfrequently insisted upon by professors of singing and elocution, and prescribed in their text-books, are undoubtedly wrong, being in direct contradiction to the general sound-law that voiced consonants (except liquids and nasals), when terminating a word, become voiceless.

FRONT-CONTINUANT-VOICE, [j]. — Same sound, flat and voiced.

English *y* in *yes, you,* if distinctly buzzed, may be identified with German [j].

German [j] is spelt: —

1. *j*, only initial in genuine German words; e. g. *ja* [jaː], yes, *Major* [ma'joːr], major.

GERMAN SOUNDS.

2. *y,* in foreign words; e. g. *Yukatan* [ju:-katan] (name), *loyal* [lo'ja:l], loyal.

3. not represented in words originally French such as *Bouteille* [bu'tɛljə], bottle, *Mignon* [mɪn'jɔ:] (name),[1] etc.

4. *g* medial, after front vowels, and after consonants (used alternatively with [g], see page 53); e. g. *Siege* [zi:jə], victories, *Berge* [bɛrjə], mountains, *regnen* (stem, *regn-*) [re:jnɔn], rain. In the suffix *ig*, followed by some inflectional termination, as e. g. in *heiliger*, or, with *i* omitted, *heil'ger*, *g* is pronounced [j] even in some districts where medial [g] generally prevails.

In Middle and South Germany, [j], except when represented in spelling by *g*, is replaced by [ɪ].

When = *g* in spelling, it is in Middle Germany not distinguished from *ch* = "*ich*-Laut." This must not be imitated.

BACK-CONTINUANT-BREATH, (x). — This sound, the "*ach*-Laut," is articulated between the back of the tongue and the middle of the soft palate, where also the vowel [u] is formed.

---

[1] Unaccented *i*, otherwise pronounced [ɪ], often becomes [j] in such words as *Familie* [fa'mi:ljə], family, *Spanien* [ʃpa:njən], Spain, etc.

It may be heard in Scotland, for *ch* in *loch*, or for the initial sound of *wh* in *what*, where however it is "labialized," the lips being rounded as in pronouncing [u].

The German [x] has the following spellings (compare *"ich*-Laut," page 55): —

1. *ch*, after back vowels; e. g. *ach* [ˀax], ah, *Buch*, [buːx], book.

2. *cch*, in some Greek or Latin names; e. g. *Bacchus* [baxʊs].

3. *g* final, after back vowels (used alternatively with [k], see page 55); e. g. *Tag* [taːx], day, *zog*, [tsoːx], drew (sing.).

BACK-CONTINUANT-VOICE, [g]. — Same sound, flat and voiced.

[g] has the same relationship to [q] as [x] has to [k].

In German it is represented only by: —

g medial, after back vowels (used alternatively with [q], see page 57); e. g. *Tage* [taːgə], days, *zogen* [tsoːgən] drew (plur.).

In Middle Germany, the "*ach*-Laut" is wrongly used instead of [g].

As to the alternative pronunciations of medial *g* as either [q] or [j] and [g], and of final *g* as either [k] or [ç] and [x], the former is used in the South of Germany and in Silesia, *as also on the stage and in the concert room all over the country;* the latter in the Midland and in the North.[1]

The second mode is still the one followed by the majority of speakers, but has been losing ground for the last ten or fifteen years, the simpler and more consistent "stop" pronunciation of *g*, especially medial [g], being gradually adopted in schools. Moreover medial [g] by the side of final [ç] and [x], e. g. in *Siege* [ziːgə], *Sieg* [ziːç], has long been employed in Hanoverian pronunciation.

THROAT CONSONANTS

THROAT-STOP-BREATH, [ʔ]. — This sound, the "glottal stop," is produced by closing and reopening the glottis with an explosion of breath, in the same manner as in coughing, only less forcibly.

The glottal stop, which is not used in English, in German regularly precedes every initial vowel, in compounds as well as in simple words.

In the usual spelling it is not represented.

E. g. *all* [ʔal], all, *überall* [ʔyːbərˈʔal], everywhere, *irren*, [ʔɪrən], err, *abirren*, [ˈʔapˈʔɪrən], swerve.

Only where a compound is no longer felt as

---

[1] In the language of the stage, *-ig* is pronounced [ɪç], except when followed by *-lich*; *-ige* etc. being [ɪgə] etc., *'ge* etc. (e. g. in *heil'ge*), [jə] etc.

such, the glottal stop is omitted, e. g. *allein* [ʔa'laɪn], alone, from *all* [ʔal], all, and *ein* [ʔaɪn], one. So also *Obacht* [ʔoːbaxt], heed, *Einöde* [ʔaɪnøːdə], desert, *daraus* [da:'raŭs], *heraus* [hɛ'raŭs], *hinaus* [hɪ'naŭs], out of it, and similar adverbs compounded with *dar, her, hin,* etc.

When a word, in speaking rapidly, is closely connected with the preceding one, it frequently loses its initial [ʔ]; especially unaccented little words such as *ich, er, es,* etc., e. g. *will ich* [vɪl ɪç], *hat er* [hat ər], *mufs es* [mʊs əs], instead of [vɪl ʔɪç], [hat ʔeːr], [mʊs ʔɛs].[1]

In various, especially South German, provincial pronunciations, the glottal stop is not used.

*** Be careful to employ the [ʔ] before every initial not altogether unaccented vowel in German. Say [ʔapʔɪrən], not [ʔapɪrən], still less [ʔabɪrən], etc.

THROAT-CONTINUANT-BREATH, [h]. — This sound, the so-called "aspirate," is formed in emitting breath through the glottis, whilst the vocal chords are sufficiently approached to each other to cause friction.

In English, the emission of breath forming the [h] is not very strong, and sensibly diminishes before the following vowel commences; whilst

---

[1] So often *'s ist* [zɪst], it is, 'tis, instead of *es ist* [ʔɛs ʔɪst].

German [h] is pronounced forcibly and is immediately connected with the following vowel, which, as may be inferred, must have some (not necessarily primary) accent.

Between vowels, in German as well in English, [h] becomes voiced, the breath passing only through the cartilage glottis, whilst the chord glottis is closed for producing voice.

The German [h]-sound is never "dropped," even by the most vulgar speakers.[1]

It is always represented by: —

h, e. g. *Hand* [hant], hand, *Ahorn* [ˀaːhɔrn], maple-tree.

⁎⁎* Pronounce German [h] strongly and shortly, avoiding the *decrescendo* effect of English [h]. Compare English *hand* [h>æn:d] with German *Hand* [hant].

---

[1] The written letter *h*, however, is very often "mute," or only serves to indicate that the following or preceding vowel is long. See the following chapter, and also the examples given on pages 8, 11, 14, 17, 18, 21, 26, 29.

THE LETTERS OF THE ALPHABET
AND THEIR PHONETIC VALUES IN GERMAN.

Having in the preceding chapter considered the German speech-sounds and their spellings, we may now try to determine in detail when a certain letter or letter-combination is to have one or another of the various pronunciations for which it may stand.

It will be useful to premise the following remarks with reference to German spelling and syllabication.

A syllable is "open," when it terminates in a vowel; it is "closed," when the last sound (or letter) is a consonant. In German syllabication, simple consonants between vowels are allotted to the second syllable, the former syllable thus remaining "open." *ſs*, *ch*, and *sch*, *ph*, *th*, *dt*, *ng*, where they represent one sound only, are treated as simple consonants.

Double consonants, and two different consonants, are divided between the two syllables, and thus the former syllable becomes "closed."

For *kk*, *ck* is written (divided *k-k*).

Digraphs and trigraphs are never doubled, *ch*, *sch*, etc., being sometimes equivalent to *chch*, *schsch*; *ng*, when not = *n-g*, always stands, so to say, for *ngng*.

In an open syllable, if not unaccented, the vowel is pronounced long; in a closed syllable, not being the last, it is pronounced short.

When a closed syllable is the last, its vowel is short if followed by more than one consonant sign, but long if followed by one only, because it becomes open as soon as an inflectional termination beginning with a vowel is added; e. g. *gut*, good, *gu-te*.

Final *ſs* = ß is in many words to be read as *ss* = ſſ, which is not used at the end of a word; e. g. *Roſs*, horse, dative case, *Ros-se*; but *Floſs*, raft, dative case, *Flo-fse*.

In word-forms that can take no inflection, and in some few that can be inflected, simple final consonants are written also after short vowels; e. g. *mit*, with.

Older loan-words from Greek and Latin on the whole comply with these rules. Stop + *l* or *r*, as well as *f* + *r*, generally both belong to the following syllable, e. g. *Atreus* = *A-treus*.

Many younger loan-words, however, especially those retaining their original spelling, form exceptions.

a.

1. = [a:] in open syllables, e. g. *da*, there, *laden*, load; and before simple final consonants; e. g. *war*, was.

Before *ſs* (when it does not stand for *ss*, but remains *ſs* before terminations beginning with a vowel) = [s] in: —

aſs,[1] ate, *fraſs*, ate, *Fraſs*, food, *maſs*, measured, *Maſs*, measure, *saſs*, sat, *Spaſs*, fun, *vergaſs*, forgot.

Before *ch* (which consequently does not stand for *chch*) = [x] in: —

brach, fallow, *brach*, broke, *nach*, after, *Schmach*, disgrace, *sprach*, spoke, *Sprache*, language, *stach*, stung.

Often before *sch* = [ʃ] in *drasch*, thrashed.

EXCEPTIONS. — Short [a] in open syllable, in interjections: *da*, there! *ja*, why! indeed!, *na*, well! and in loan-words such as: —

Araber,[2] Arab, *AttAque*, attack, *Claque*, claque, *Fiaker*,[3] cab, *GAla*, gala, *GrammAtik*, grammar, *grammAtisch*, grammatical, *KAkadu*, cockatoo, *KAnapee*, sofa, *KAnevas*, canvas, *Metapher*, metaphor, *Paletot*, paletot, *Saphir*, sapphire, *Tschako*, shako.

Also short vowel in *Atlas*, *SAfran*.

Short [a] before simple final consonant, mostly in words that cannot be inflected, and loan-words: —

---

[1] Compounds, derivatives, etc., always included.
[2] [ʔarabər]. But, *arabisch* [ʔa'raːbɪʃ].
[3] [fi'akər]. Also pronounced [fiːakər].

THE LETTERS OF THE ALPHABET.

ab, of, *am* = *an dem*, at the, *an*, at, on, *As*, ace, A flat, *Bamberg* (name), *Dam-*, in *Damhirsch*, fallow deer, *das*, that, the, *Ham*, Ham (name), *Hamburg* (name), *hat*, has, *man*, one, *Mar-*, in *Marstall*, (royal) mews, *Marbach*, *Marburg* (names), *Wal-*, in *Walnufs*, walnut, *Walfisch*, whale, *was*, what.

In unaccented syllables, in *Nektar*, nectar, *Seraph*, seraph, *Tombak*, pinchbeck, *Vivat*, cheer, and generally in *Bisam*, musk, *Bräutigam*, bridegroom, *Eidam*, son-in-law, *Islam*, Islam.

2. = [a] in closed syllables (page 62); e. g. *warten*, wait, *all*, all.

EXCEPTIONS. — Long [a:] in closed syllable[1] in: *Arlberg*[2] (name), *Arnsberg*[2] (name), *Art*, manner, *Arzt*, physician, *Bart*, beard, *Bratsche*, viol, *Glatz* (name), *Gratz* (name), *Hardt* (name), *Harz*, resin (also name), *Jagd*, hunting, *Kap*, cape, *Kladderadatsch* (name of comic paper), *Karbatsche*, lash, *Magd*, maid, *Papst*, pope, *Quarz*, quartz, *Schwarte*, skin of bacon, *Starnberg*[2] (name), *Start*, start, *zart*, tender.

Unaccented in *Hoffart*, haughtiness.

---

[1] Also in *Adler*, because rather = *A-dler*, than *Ad-ler*.

[2] Short [a], where the correct local pronunciation is not known. Also in most of the other words short [a] frequently heard. Always [a:] in *Papst*.

aa.[1]

1. Regularly = [aː]: —
Aal, eel, *Aar*, eagle (and name), *Aas*, carrion, *Haar*, hair, *Paar*, pair, *(ein) paar*, some, *Saal*, hall, *Saat*, seed, *Staat*, state.

2. = [a], sometimes in *Isaak* [ʔiːzak], Isaac.

ah.

Always = [aː]; e. g. *nah*, near, *fahnden*, search.

ai.

1. = [aɪ] in German words and naturalized loan-words:
Bai, bay, frith, *Hai*, shark, *Hain*, grove, *Kaiser*, emperor, *Laib*, loaf, *Laich*, spawn, *Laie*, layman, *Lakai*, lackey, *Mai*, May, *Maid*, maiden, *Mais*, maize, *Maisch*, mash, *Rain*, ridge of land, *Saite*, string, *Waid*, woad, *Waise*, orphan;

also in German or Germanized names, as *Mailand*, Milan, *Main*, *Maier*, etc., and followed by mute *l*, in French words in *-ail*, where [aɪ] is very nearly the original pronunciation; e. g. *Detail*, detail; similarly *-ailles* in *Versailles* (name).[2]

---

[1] i. e. *aa* as a digraph. No notice is taken of words like *Baal* (name), *Barlaam* (name), where either *a* has its separate value. Similarly in the following sections.

[2] Yet, as French "*l* mouillé" is generally taken for

THE LETTERS OF THE ALPHABET. 67

2. = [ɛː], in French words, where *ai* is thus pronounced in French; e. g. *Palais*, palace.

ain.

Pronounced [ɛ̃ː] in French loan-words such as *Train*, baggage (of an army). North German — not, however, stage — pronunciation, [ɛŋ].

am, an.

Pronounced [ãː] in French loan-words such as *Chance*, chance. North German pronunciation, [aŋ].

Not when *am* is followed by a lip-stop, or *an* by a point-stop: — *Champagner* [ʃamˈpanjər], champagne; *Gouvernante* [guvɛrˈnantə], governess; *Girlande* [gɪrˈlandə], garland. — *Bankier* [baŋkˈjeː], banker.

au.

1. = [aŭ] in all really German words; e. g. *Au*, lea.
2. = [oː] in French loan-words; e. g. *Sauce*, now also *Soſse*, sauce.

aw.

Pronounced [aː] in the English loan-word *Shawl*, now *Schal*, shawl.

[lj], and final voiced [j] becomes voiceless [ç] according to a German sound-law mentioned before, [deˈtalç], [vɛrˈzalç], instead of [deˈtaɪ̯], [vɛrˈsaɪ̯], etc., are frequently heard, especially in the North. This must not be imitated.

5*

ay.

1. = [aɪ], only used in names; e. g. *Bayern*, Bavaria, *Mayer* (name).
2. = [ɛː] in loan-words such as *Essay*,[1] essay.

ä.

1. = [ɛː] in open syllables; e. g. *säen*, sow; and before simple final consonants; e. g. *Bär*, bear.

Before *fs* final (not standing for *ss*) = [s] in: *Gefäfs*, vessel, *Gefräfs*, food for beasts, *gemäfs*, according to, *Gesäfs*, seat, bottom.

Before *ch* (not standing for *chch*) = [x] in *Gespräch*, conversation; also in *nächst* (stem, *näch*), next.

Before *dt* = [t] in *Städte*, towns. As the singular *Stadt* is invariably pronounced with short [a], the Middle and South German short [ɛ] in *Städte* seems more correct than the North German [ɛː], which, however, prevails on the stage.

2. = [ɛ] in closed syllables; e. g. *Hände*, hands.

EXCEPTIONS. — Long [ɛː] in closed syllable in: *grätschen*, straddle, *hätscheln*, caress, *Kardätsche*, card (comb), *Kartätsche*, cartridge, *trätschen*, prate.

---

[1] Pronounced [ˀɛsɛː]; by many speakers, [ˀɛ'sɛː], [ˀɛ'sεː].

äh.

Invariably = [ɛː]; e. g. *mähen*, mow; *Ähre*, ear (of corn).

äu.

Always = [ɔÿ]; e. g. *gläubig*, believing, *Bäume*, trees.

b.

1. = [b], initial or medial, i. e. followed by a vowel, or by a liquid consonant (*l, m, n, r*) forming part of the stem of the word, an unaccented *e* = [ə] generally being omitted before the liquid; e. g. *Bahn*, track, *Liebe*, love, *übler* (stem, *übl, übel*), worse.

2. = [p], final, also when followed by a liquid not belonging to the stem, or by any other consonant; e. g. *ab*, off, *liebt*, loves, *üblich* (stem, *üb*) customary. There is another word *üblich*, sickly, standing for *übellich*, where *b* is pronounced [b], (see under 1).

bb.

Pronounced [b], preceding vowel short; e. g. *Ebbe*, ebb.

c.

1. Regularly = [ts] before front vowels; e. g. *Cis*, C sharp.[1] So also before *k* in Polish names, as *Potocki*.

---

[1] So also in *Officier* (= *Offizier*), officer. There is an affected pronunciation, = [ʔɔfi'siːr], which must be avoided.

2. Regularly = [k] in other cases, i. e. before back vowels, before consonants, and final; e. g. *Cognac*, or *Kognak*, cognac.

3. = [s] before front vowels, in French words; e. g. *Annonce* [ʔa'nɔ̃:sə], advertisement.

4. = [tʃ] before front vowels, in Italian words; e. g. *Cicerone*,[1] cicerone. In *Cello*, *Violoncell*, violoncello, *Cellist*, violoncellist, *c* is commonly pronounced [ʃ]: [ʃɛlo:], [violɔ̃:'ʃɛl], [ʃɛ'lıst].

cc.

1. = [kts] before front vowels; e. g. *Accent*, or *Akzent*, [ʔak'tsɛnt], accent. New spelling, *kz*.

2. = [k] before back vowels; e. g. *Accord*, or *Akkord*, [ʔa'kɔrt], accord. New spelling, *kk*.

cch.

Pronounced [x] in some Greek and Latin words; e. g. *Bacchus*, *Gracchus*.

cci.

Pronounced [tʃ] in a few Italian loan-words; e. g. *Kapriccio*, capriccio; often, however, the *i* is pronounced separately, = [ɪ], [j].

ch.

1. = [ç] after front vowels, and after consonants; e. g. *ich*, I, *solch*, such, *manch*, many a, *Pferch*, fold, pen; and *always* in the derivative syllable *chen*; e. g. *Papachen*, dear papa, *Frauchen*, little woman.

---

[1] [tʃitʃə'ro:nə]; but [tsitsə'ro:nə] is frequent.

Also initial, in the following and similar foreign words: —
Chalcis, Chalcis, *Chares* (name), *Charis* (name), *Charon* (name), *Chäronea*, Chæronea, *Charybdis*, (name), *Chauker*, Chauci, *Chemie*, chemistry, *Cheops* (name), *Cherson* (name), *Chersonnes*, Chersonesus, *Cherub*, cherub, *Cherusker*, Cherusci, *Chiasma*, chiasma, *Chimäre*, chimera, *China*, China, *Chios* (name), *Chiron* (name), *Chirurg*, surgeon, *Chlamys*, chlamys, *Chrie*, chria, *Chrysostomus*, Chrysostom, *chthonisch*, chthonian.

In the Old German names *Childerich*, *Chilperich*, *ch* is also pronounced [ç].

2. = [x] after back vowels, e. g. *ach*, ah, *rauchen*, smoke.

3. = [k], when followed by radical *s* = [s], in the following German words: —

Achse, axle, *Achsel*, shoulder, *Buchs*, in *Buchsbaum*, boxwood, *Büchse*, box, rifle, *Dachs*, badger, *Deichsel*, pole, *drechseln*, turn (on a lathe), *Eidechse*, lizard, *Fechser*, layer, bud, *Flachs*, flax, *Flechse*, sinew, *Fuchs*, fox, *Lachs*, salmon, *Luchs*, lynx, *Ochse*, ox, *Sachse*, Saxon, *sechs*, six (not in *sechzehn*, *sechzig*), *wachsen*, grow, *wechseln*, change, *Weichsel*, Vistula, *Wichse*, blacking.

Also in *Chatten*, Chatti, *Chemnitz*, *Chlodwig*, *Chur* (names), and the following and some other words, not originally German:

Chalcedon,[1] chalcedony, *Chaldäa*, Chaldæa, *Chamäleon*, chameleon, *Chan* (also *Khan*), khan, *Chaos*, chaos (or [ça:ɔs]), *Charakter*, character, *Chloe* (name), *Chlor*, chlorine, *Chlorus* (name), *Cholera*, cholera, *Chor*, choir, *Chrestomathie*, anthology, *Chrysam*, chrism, *Christ(us)*, Christian, Christ, *Chrom*, chromium, *Chronik*, chronicle.

So also in Italian loan-words; e. g. *Scherzo*, scherzo.

4. = [ʃ] in French loan-words, of which the following are among the most common, with *ch* initial: —

Chaine, chain, *Chaise*, carriage, *chamois*, chamois, *Champagner* [ʃam'panjər], champagne, *Champignon*, champignon, *Chance*, chance, *changieren*, change, *Charge*, commission, *Charlaian*, charlatan, *Charlotte* (name), *charmant*, charming, *Charpie*, lint, *Chaussee*, high road, *Chef*, principal, *Chemisett*, shirt-front, *chevaleresk*, chivalrous, *Chicane* (= *Schikane*), chicane, *Chiffre*, cipher, *Chignon*, chignon, *Chimäre* (= *Schimäre*), chimera, *Chock*, shock.

5. = [tʃ], in a few foreign words; e. g. *Guttapercha*, guttapercha [gʊta'pɛrtʃa:], often however [gʊta'pɛrça:].

ck.

Pronounced [k], after short vowel; e. g. *dick*, thick.

---

[1] = [kal'tse:dɔn]. When name of town, = [çal'tse:dɔn].

cqu.

Pronounced [kv]; e. g. *Acquisition*, acquisition. New spelling, *kqu*.

ç.

Always = [s] in French loan-words; e. g. *Façon*, shape.

d.

1. = [d], initial and medial; e. g. *du*, thou, *drei*, three, *Hände*, hands.
2. = [t], final; e, g. *Hand*, hand, *handlich*, handy.
3. Mute in French words such as *Fonds*, fund.

dd.

Pronounced [d], after short vowel, e. g. *Kladde*, rough note-book.

dt.

Pronounced [t]; e. g. *Stadt*, town, *wandte*, turned.

e.

1. = [e:] in open syllables (apart from cases mentioned under 4); e. g. *ade* [ˀa'de:], farewell, *Rede*, speech; and before simple final consonants; e. g. *schwer*, heavy.

EXCEPTIONS. — Short [ɛ] before *ph* = [f] in *Stephan*, Stephen, and before simple final consonant in: —

Billet,[1] note, *Bouquet*,[1] bouquet, *Chef*, head, principal, *Des*, D flat, *des*, of the, etc., *es*, it, *Gebhard* (name), *gen*, towards, *Hotel*, hotel, *Lemberg* (name), *Reb-*, in *Rebhuhn*, partridge, *Relief*, relief, *Sem*, Shem, *weg*, away, *wes*, of what, etc., and other foreign words, similar to those quoted.

In unaccented final syllables, in: —
Achilles (name), etc., *amen*, amen, *Debet*, debet, *Elen*, elk, *Joseph* (name), *Requiem*, Requiem, *Tibet*, Thibet.

2. = [ɛː] in French words where this is the French sound; e. g. *Dessert*, dessert, *Karriere*, career.

3. = [ɛ] in closed syllables (apart from cases under 4); e. g. *fest*, fast.

EXCEPTIONS. — Long [eː] in closed syllable in: *Beschwerde*, trouble, *Dresden* (name), *Ems* (name of town),[2] *Erde*, earth, *erst*, first, *Erz*, ore, *Esthen*, Esths, *Estland*, Esthonia, *Geberde*, gesture, *Hedwig* (name), *Herd*, hearth, *Herde*, flock, *Kebs-*, in *Kebsweib*, concubine, *Krebs*, crayfish, *Mecklenburg* (name), *nebst*,

---

[1] = [bɪl'jɛt], [bu'kɛt], now spelt *Billett*, *Bukett*. In most words in *et* the *et* is pronounced [eɪt]; e. g. *Paket* [pa'keɪt], packet, etc. For *Budget*, budget, see page 14.

[2] By North Germans wrongly pronounced [ʔɛms], like the name of the river *Ems* in Hanover. This has been of late foolishly imitated by the inhabitants themselves.

together with, *Pegnitz* (name), *Pferd*, horse, *Quedlinburg* (name), *Schwedt* (name), *Schwert*, sword, *Schwetz* (name), *stets*, always, *Teplitz* (name), *Verden* (name), *Werden* (name), *werden*, become, *wert*, worth, dear, *-werth*, in *Kaiserswerth* (name), etc.[1]

4. = [ə] in the unaccented prefixes *be-* and *ge*, and in the unaccented derivative or inflectional suffixes *e*,[2] *el*, *em*, *en*, *end*,[3] *er*, *ern*, *es*, *est*, *et*, also combined, *ele*, etc.; e. g. *habe*, have, *Vogel*, bird, *Atem*, breath, *lieben*, love, *rasend*, furious, *Vater*, father, *eisern*, iron, *alles*, all, *leidet*, suffers, *ich handele*, I act, etc.

Similarly, unaccented *e* in cases like *Karneval*, carnival, etc. becomes [ə].

The *e* in *der*, the, *dem*, (to) the, *den*, the, *des*, of the, *es*, it, when unaccented, is also pronounced [ə].

eau.

Pronounced [oː] in French loan-words; e. g. *Plateau*, plateau.

---

[1] In many of these words also [ɛ] is in use.

[2] Also "mute" final *e* French loan-words which in German are of the masculine or of feminine gender (except after vowels); e. g. *Chance*, chance.

[3] Not in *Elend*, misery, *elend*, miserable, which both = [ʔeːlɛnt]. As to *el*, *em*, *en*, *es*, see exceptions under *e* 1, page 74 f.

ee.

1. = [eː]; e. g. *Beet*, flower-bed.[1]
2. = [iː] in English loan-words; e. g. *Beefsteak*,[2] beef-steak.

eh.

Apart from provincial pronunciations invariably = [eː]; e. g. *Reh*, roe, *stehlen*, steal.

ei.

1. = [aɪ]; e. g. *Ei*, egg, *Seil*, rope.
2. = [ɛɪ], with mute *l*, in French words in *eil*, such as *Conseil*, council.[3]

ein.

Pronounced [ɛ̃ː] in French loan-words such as *Pleinpouvoir*, liberty of action.[4]

em, en.

Pronounced [ãː] in French loan-words such as *Trente-et-un*, trente-et-un.[5]

---

[1] Unaccented in the naturalized loan-word *Kaffee* [kafeː], coffee. But *Café* [kaˈfeː], coffee-house.

[2] Perhaps most commonly pronounced [biːfstɛk]; but there are many variations.

[3] North German pronunciation, [ɛlç].

[4] North German pronunciation, [ɛŋ].

[5] Also in *Pension* [pãːsˈɪoːn], pension, boarding-house. But *ennuyiren* [ʔanyˈjiːrən], tire. North German pronunciation [aŋ].

eu.

1. = [ɔy̆]; e. g. *Heu*, hay, *Leute*, people.
2. = [øː] in French loan-words: e. g. *adieu*, good bye, *Redakteur*, editor.

ey.

Pronounced [aɪ] in names; e. g. *Meyer*.

é.

Always = [eː]; only used in foreign words, for the modern *ee*, and in secondarily accented syllables of names where simple *e* would be read as [ə]; e. g. *Jungé*.

f.

Invariably = [f]; e. g. *Fall*, fall, *Lauf*, run.

ff.

Always = [f], after short vowels; e. g. *Schiff*, ship, *hoffen*, hope.

g.

1. = [g], initial, and in foreign words when beginning the primarily accented syllable; e. g. *gut*, good, *regieren*, reign, *Regress*, regress.
2. = [g] or [j], medial, after front vowels, and after consonants; e. g. *Siege*, victories, *Berge*, mountains, *regnen*, rain.
3. = [g] or [g], medial, after back vowels; e. g. *Tage*, days, *zogen*, drew.

4. = [ʒ], initial and medial, in the following and some other loan-words: —

Adagio,[1] adagio, *Agio*,[1] agio, *arrangieren*, arrange, *Baggage*, luggage, *Bandage*, bandage, *changieren*, change, *Charge*, commission, rank, *Doge*, doge, *Eloge*, praise, eulogy, *Gage*, salary, *Gelee*, jelly, *Gendarm*,[2] constable, *generös*, generous, *Genie*, genius, ingenuity[3], *genieren*, constrain, *Genre*,[4] kind, *Ingenieur*,[5] engineer, *Negligé*, negligee, *Orange*, orange, *Page*, page (boy), *Regie*,[6] administration, *voltigieren*, vault.

5. = [dʒ], often simply [ʒ], initial, in English and Italian words; e. g. *Gentleman*, *Giro*, giro.

6. = [k], final in *flugs*, quickly, and in foreign words such as *Log*, log.

7. = [k] or [ç], final, after front vowels, and after consonants; e. g. *Sieg*, victory, *Berg*, mountain, *regsam*, active.

8. = [k] or [x], final, after back vowels; e. g. *Tag*, day, *zog*, drew, *Wagnis*, perilous enterprise.

gg.

1. = [ɡ], medial; e. g. *Flagge*, flag.
2. = [k], final; e. g. *Brigg*, brig.

---

[1] Mostly [ʔaˈdaɪʒĭoɪ], [ʔaɪʒĭoɪ]. The [ĭ] is better omitted.

[2] [ʒanˈdarm].

[3] Not in *genial*, full of genius, *Genius*, genius, spirit, where *g* = [ɡ].

[4] [ʒãːr].

[5] [ʔɪnʒenĭˈøːr].

[6] Not in *regieren*, reign (see page 77).

ggi.

Pronounced [dʒ] in Italian words such as *Arpeggio*, arpeggio. Often = [dʒɪ].

ge.

Pronounced [ʒ] in French loan-words such as *Flageolett*, flageolet, *Sergeant*, sergeant.

gn.

Besides [gn], [jn], [ŋn], and [çn], [xn] (for which see pronunciation of *g*): —

1. Often = [ŋn], in words originally Latin, or treated as such; e. g. *Magnat*, magnate, *Agnes* (name), Otherwise [gn].

2. = [nj], in words originally French; e. g. *Mignon* (name).[1]

gu.

Pronounced [g] in the following and some other foreign words:

Guerilla,[2] guerilla, *Guido*, Guy, *Guillotine*, guillotine, *Guinea*[2] (name), *Guinee*,[2] guinea, *Guipüre*, guipure, *Guirlande*,[2] garland, *Guitarre*, guitar (the last three now spelt with *g*); and in French loan-words in *gue*; e. g. *Drogue*, drug, *Intrigue*, intrigue[3] (both now spelt with *g*).

---

[1] Also in *Compagnon* [kɔmpan'jɔɪ], partner, but not in *Compagnie* (= *Kompanie*) [kompa'niː], company.

[2] [gɛ'rɪljaɪ], [gɪljo'tiːnə], [gi'neːaɪ], [gi'neː], [gɪr'landə].

[3] [droːgə], [ʔɪn'triːgə].

h.

Pronounced [h] when followed by a vowel that does not commence a suffix, and when not forming part of a digraph such as *ch*, *th*, etc. E. g. *Hand*, hand, *Ahorn*, maple-tree. Compare also *ha*, etc.

ha (h-a) etc.; new spelling, a.

After *t*, instead of *ah*, etc., *ha* (*h-a*), etc. are written; e. g. *Thal*, valley, *Thran*, train-oil, *Thor*, fool, gate, etc. The pronunciation is the same as that of *ah*, etc. See also *th*.

i.

1. = [i:] in open syllables; e. g. *Igel*, hedgehog; and before simple final consonants; e. g. *mir*, me.

Before *sch* (which consequently is not meant for *schsch*) = [ʃ], in *Nische*, niche.

EXCEPTIONS. — Short [ɪ] mostly pronounced in open syllable in *Clique*, clique, and always in *Kapitel*, chapter, *Zither*, (musical instrument).

Short [ɪ] before simple final consonant in:
April, April, *bin*, am, *bis*, till, as far as, *Cis*, C sharp[1], *Him-*, in *Himbeere*, raspberry, *hin*, thither, *mit* with, *im* = *in dem*, in the; *in*, in, *Ir-*, in *Irland*, Ireland, *Krim*, Crimea, *Limburg* (name), *Schwib-*, in *Schwibbogen*, vaulted arch, *Sin-*, in *Singrün*, periwinkle, *Winfried* (name);

---

[1] And similar musical terms: *Dis*, D sharp, etc.

also in the unaccented suffixes *ib* (*Wittib* = *Witwe*, widow), *ich* (*lich, rich*), *ig, in, is, isch*, and *nis*;[1] e. g. *Bottich*, vat, *Käfig*, cage, *Königin*, queen, *Firnis*, varnish, *Harnisch*, armour, *Ereignis*, event; and in unaccented *ik, ir, it*; e. g. *Poetik*,[2] art of poetry, *Deficit*, deficiency, *Saphir*, sapphire.

Mostly also *im* in *Pilgrim*, pilgrim, and always in names such as *Joachim, Arnim*.

2. = [ɪ], in closed syllables; *Kiste*, chest.

3. = [ɪ], [j], before [ə]; e. g. *Familie*, family, *Spanien*, Spain.

Compare *ai, ei, oi, ui*, etc.

ie.

1. = [i:]; e. g. *sie*, she, *Liebe*, love. So also in many words of foreign origin in *ie*, mostly abstract nouns, names of sciences, etc. from French; e. g.: —

Akademie, academy, *Anarchie*, anarchy, *Anatomie*, anatomy, *Aristokratie*, aristocracy, *Artillerie*, artillery, *Astronomie*, astronomy, *Demokratie*, democracy, *Energie*, energy, *Epidemie*, epidemic, *Gallerie*, gallery, *Garantie*, warranty, *Genie*,

---

[1] In the plural the *n* or *s* is doubled, according to the general rule; e. g. *Königinnen, Ereignisse*.

[2] Provincially (in the Middle and South of Germany) also accented *ik, ip, it, iz*, as in *Musik*, music, *Prinzip*, principle, *Granit*, granite, *Hospiz*, hospice, etc., are pronounced with short [ɪ] instead of [i:].

genius, *Geographie*, geography, *Geometrie*, geometry, *Harmonie*, harmony, *Industrie*, industry, *Infanterie*, infantry, *Kolonie*, colony, *Kompanie*, company, *Kopie*, copy, *Lotterie*, lottery, *Melodie*, melody, *Orthographie*, orthography, *Partie*, party, part, *Phantasie*, phantasy, *Philologie*, philology, *Philosophie*, philosophy, *Poesie*, poetry, *Symmetrie*, symmetry, *Sympathie*, sympathy, *Telegraphie*, telegraphy, *Theologie*, theology, divinity, *Theorie*, theory;

in all verbs ending in *ieren*, e. g.: —
regieren, reign, *spazieren*, go for a walk;

and in most nouns in *ier*, e. g.: —
Barbier, barber, *Kanonier*, gunner, *Klavier*, piano, *Manier*, manner, *Quartier*, quarter.

2. = [iːə], but often only [iː], in: —
Marie, Mary, *Sophie*, Sophia.

3. = [ĭə], [jə]; in many nouns in *ie*, mostly taken from Latin; e. g : —
Aktie, share, *Familie*, family, *Furie*, fury, *Glorie*, glory, *Grazie*, grace, *Historie*, history, *Injurie*, insult, *Kurie*, curie, *Linie*, line, *Materie*, matter, *Mumie*, mummy, *Prämie*, premium, *Reliquie*, relic;

in names of plants such as
Cichorie, chicory, *Fuchsie*, fuchsia;

in Christian names such as
Amalie, Amelia, *Emilie*, Emily, *Lucie*, Lucy;

in names of countries in *ien*, e. g.: —
Belgien, Belgium, *Indien*, India, *Spanien*, Spain, etc.,
(so also: —
Belgier, Belgian, *Spanier*, Spaniard, etc.),
and in nouns in *ien* only used in the plural, e. g.: —
Ferien, holidays, *Mobilien*, furniture, etc.

4. = [ɪeː], [jeː], in foreign words such as *Diego* (name), *Gabriele*, Gabriella, *Hygiene*, hygiene;
also in French words in *ier* where *ier* retains its French pronunciation (*r* silent), e. g.: —
Atelier, studio, *Bankier*, banker, *Metier*, trade, *Portier*, porter.

5. = [ɪɛː], [jɛː], in French words where *iè* is the French spelling; e. g.: —
Barriere, barrier, *Karriere*, career, *Tantieme*, royalty, share.

6. = [ɪɛ], [jɛ], in foreign words such as *Patient*, patient, *Audienz*, audience, *speziell*, special, *Serviette*, napkin, *Triennium*, space of three years.

7. = [ɪ], in: —
Viertel, quarter, fourth, *vierzehn*, fourteen, *vierzig*, forty;
also sometimes unaccented in *vielleicht*, perhaps.

ieh.

Always = [iː]; e. g. *Vieh*, cattle, *stiehlt*, steals.

ieu.

Pronounced [ɔÿ] in *Lieutenant* (new spelling, *Leutnant*), lieutenant.

ih.

Pronounced [i:] in: —
ihm, ihn, him, *ihnen,* them, *ihr,* her, their; you, *ihrer,* of her, of them, *ihrig,* hers, theirs.

il.

Pronounced [ĭ] in French words such as *Detail,* detail, *Fauteuil,* easy-chair.[1]

ill (ll).

Pronounced [lj] in French words such as *Bouteille,* bottle, *Medaillon,* medallion, *Postill(i)on,* postillion[2].

im, in.

Pronounced [ɛ̃:] in French words such as *Bassin,* basin.[3]

j.

1. Regularly = [j]; e. g. *ja,* yes, *Major,* major.

2. = [ʒ], in the following and some similar words: —

---

[1] North German pronunciation, [de'talç], [fo'tœlç].
[2] [bu'tɛljə], [medal'jɔ:], [postɪl'jo:n].
[3] North German pronunciation, [ba'sɛŋ].

Jalousie, Venetian blinds, *Jargon*, jargon, *Jenny* (name), *Journal*, journal, *Don Juan*[1] (name).

Jasmin, jasmine, has mostly (j) in North German pronunciation.

3. = [dʒ], for which, however, [ʒ] is commonly substituted, in a few English words: —

Jockey, jockey, *Jury*, jury,

the latter often being pronounced in the German way, with *j* = [j].

k.

Invariably = [k]; e. g. *kahl*, bald.

l.

Pronounced [l]; e. g. *lahm*, lame. See *il*.

ll.

Pronounced [l]; e. g. *voll*, full. See *ill*.

m.

Pronounced [m]; e. g. *mir*, me. See *am*, *em*, etc.

mm.

Invariably = [m]; e. g. *Lamm*, lamb.

n.

1. = [n]; e. g. *nie*, never, *an*, at. See *an*, etc.

2. = [ŋ]. See *ng* and *nk*.

---

[1] = [dɔ̃:ʒuã:]. North German pronunciation, [dɔŋʒuaŋ].

ng.

1. = [ŋ]; e. g. *singen*, sing, *lang*, long.
2. = [ŋg], when *ng* is followed by a vowel other than *e* = [ə] or by a consonant and such a vowel; mostly in Old German or foreign names; e. g.

Ingo, Albalonga, Ganges,[1] *Ingraban.*

nk.

Pronounced [ŋk]; e. g. *sinken*, sink, *Dank*, thanks.

nn.

Pronounced [n]; e. g. *Mann*, man. See *en*.

o.

1. = [o:] in open syllables; e. g. *so*, so, *Rose*, rose; and before simple final consonants; e. g. *Gebot*, commandment.

Before *ſs* (when it does not stand for *ss*) = [s] in: —

bloſs, bare, *Floſs*, raft, *groſs*, great, *Kloſs*, dumpling, *Stoſs*, thrust.

Before *ch* (not standing for *chch*) = [x] in *hoch*, high.[2]

---

[1] = [gaŋgɛs], the river Ganges; but *Ganges*, genitive of *Gang*, = [gaŋəs].

[2] But *Hochzeit*, wedding, *Hochheim* (name), with short [ɔ].

EXCEPTIONS. — Short [ɔ] in open syllable in loan-words, such as *Berloque*, now *Berlocke*, trinket, *Joli* (name of dog).

Often [ɔ] in syllables preceding the accented one, e. g.: —

Koloſs, colossus, *Komitee*, committee, *Pomade*, pomatum, *Pomeranze*, orange, *Promenade*, promenade, *Volontär*, volunteer.

Short [ɔ] before simple final consonant in: —

Brom-, in *Brombeere*, blackberry, *Bromberg* (name), *Chok*, shock, *Don*, don (also name), *grob*,[1] coarse (often), *Grog*,[2] grog, *Gros*, gross, *Jot*, letter J, *Lor-*, in *Lorbeer*, laurel, *Mob*,[2] mob, *ob*,[3] if, *Top*, top, *vom = von dem*, of the, *von*, of, *vor* in *Vorteil*, advantage,

and in unaccented final syllables; e. g. *Jakob*, Jacob, *Nabob*, and many words in *or, os*; e. g. *Doktor*, doctor, *Chaos*, chaos.

2. = [ɔ], in closed syllables; e. g. *Gott*, God.

EXCEPTIONS. — Long [o:] in closed syllable in: —

Jost (name), *Kloster*, convent, *Lotse*, pilot, *Mond*, moon, *Obst*, fruit, *Ostern*, Easter, *Propst*,

---

[1] Also in *Grobheit*, coarseness, *Grobschmid*, blacksmith. Not, however, in *grobe*, etc., *Grobian*, brute.

[2] Pronounced [grɔk], [mɔp].

[3] But *Obacht*, heed, *beobachten*, observe = [ʔo:baxt], [bəʔo:baxtən].

provost, *Thorn* (name), *Trost*, consolation[1], *Vogt*, bailiff, reeve.

Also in *Fort*, fort, *Ressort*, department, with mute *t*, and similar French loan-words.[2]

oa.

Pronounced [oː] in English words, as *Toast*, toast, sometimes pronounced [toʼast]. Also in *Coaks*, new spelling, *Koks*, coke.

oe.

Pronounced [oː] in Low German names; e. g. *Koesfeld, Soest;* unaccented in *Itzehoe*.

oeu.

Pronounced [øː] in the French loan-word *Coeur*, hearts (at cards).

oh.

Invariably = [oː]; e. g. *roh*, raw, *Ohr*, ear.

oi.

1. = [ɔy̆] in a few words originally English or Low German; e. g.: —
ahoi, ahoy, *Boi*, buoy, *Boizenburg* (name).

2. = [oː] in Low German names; e. g.: —
Grevenbroich, Troisdorf, Voigt (Voigtland).

---

[1] Often also in *Rost*, grill (not in *Rost*, rust).
[2] Observe, however, *Lord*, lord, = [lɔrt].

3. = [oaː] in French loan-words; e. g. *Boudoir*, boudoir;[1] = [oa] in *chamois*, chamois.

om, on.

Pronounced [õː] in French words such as *Ballon*, balloon.[2]

oo.

Pronounced [oː] in: —
Boot, boat, *Moor*, moor, *Moos*, moss.

ou.

Used in French words and pronounced the same as German *u*: —

1. = [uː] in open syllables; e. g. *Route*, route; and before simple final consonants; e. g. *Tour*, tour.

2. = [u] in closed syllables; e. g. *Ressource*, resource. *Douche*, now *Dusche*, douche, rather with [uː].

ö.

1. = [œː] in open syllables; e. g. *öde*, desert; and before simple final consonants; e. g. *schön*, beautiful.

2. = [œ] in closed syllables; e. g. *Mörder*, murderer.

---

[1] *Comptoir* (= *Kontor*) is mostly pronounced [kɔn'toːr].
[2] North German pronunciation, [ɔŋ]. Not [õː] in feminine words in *ion*, such as *Nation*, nation, where *on* is pronounced [oːn]. So also e. g. *Bataillon* = [batal'joːn], batallion, *Eskadron* = [ʔɛska'droːn], squadron.

EXCEPTIONS. — Long [ø:] in closed syllable in: —

Behörde, authority, *-förde*, in *Eckernförde* (name), etc., *Flöz*, layer, stratum, *Österreich*, *Östreich*, Austria, *Wörth* (name), also in *Donauwörth*, etc.

öh.

Invariably = [ø:]; e. g. *Höhle*, cavern.

ow.

Pronounced [o:] in the loan-word *Bowle*, bowl, and unaccented in Low German (originally Slavonic) names in *ow*, as *Bülow*, *Grabow*.

p.

1. Regularly = [p]; e. g. *Paar*, pair.
2. Mute in French loan-words such as *Coup*, coup.

ph.

Pronounced [f] in words originally Greek; e. g. *Philosophie*, philosophy.[1]

pp.

Invariably = [p]; e. g. *Rappe*, black horse, *Trupp*, troop, hord.

pph.

Pronounced [f] in the Greek name *Sappho*.

---

[1] The German word *Epheu*, ivy, is now spelt *Efeu*.

qu.

1. Regularly = [kv]; e. g. *Quelle*, spring, *bequem*, convenient.

2. = [k], in some French and other loan-words; e. g. *Claque*, claque, *Clique*, clique, *Marquis*, marquis.

r.

1. Regularly = [r]; e. g. *rauh*, rough, *hier*, here.

2. Mute in French words in *er* such as *Diner*, dinner, and some words in *ier* (see *ie*).

rh.

Pronounced [r], in Greek words; e. g. *Rhabarber*, rhubarb.

rr.

Always = [r], after a short vowel; e. g. *Narr*, fool, *verwirren*, confound.

rrh.

Pronounced [r], the preceding vowel short; in Greek words; e. g. *Katarrh*, cold.

s.

1. = [z], initial before vowels, and medial before vowels, or liquids originally preceded by *e* = [ə]; e. g. *so*, so, *Rose*, rose, *winsle* (= *winsele*), whine.

2. = [s], initial before consonants, medial before (most) consonants, and final; e. g. *Skizze*, sketch, *ist*, is, *Hals*, neck.

3. [ʃ], initial, in the combinations *sp* and *st*, and also when preceded by German prefixes; e. g. *sprechen*, speak, (*besprechen*, speak about), *stehen*, stand, (*verstehen*, understand), *spekulieren*, speculate, *studieren*, study.

In naturalized loan-words [ʃp] and [ʃt] are frequently used also after foreign prefixes; e. g. in *Inspektor*, inspector, *konstatieren*, state, affirm, etc., but this cannot yet be recommended.

In modern foreign names, except familiar ones such as

Spinoza, Staffa, Stambul, Stuart,

initial *sp* and *st* are pronounced [sp] and [st].

4. Mute in French words such as *Marquis*, marquis.

sch.

1. Regularly = [ʃ]; e. g. *scharf*, sharp, *mischen*, mix.

2. = [sk] in Italian words, e. g. *Scherzo*, scherzo.

sh.

Pronounced [ʃ] in English words; e. g. *Shawl*, [ʃaːl], shawl, *Sherry*, sherry; also in *S(c)hlips*, neck-tie.

ſs (ß), ss (ſſ).

Both invariably = [s]; e. g. *Fuſs*, foot, *Kasse*, cash.

t.

1. Regularly = [t]; e. g. *Tau*, rope, *warten*, wait, *mit*, with.

2. = [ts] before unaccented *i* followed by an accented vowel in words originally Latin; e. g. *Nation*, nation, *Patient*, patient; followed by unaccented *e* = [ə] in *Aktie*, share,[1] and *en* = [ən], as in *Böotien*, Bœotia.

3. Mute in French words such as
Depot, depot, *Budget*, budget, *Arrangement*, arrangement.

th.

Always = [t]; in German words formerly occurring through transposition of the letter *h* when used to indicate length of a neighbouring vowel, e. g. *Thal* (compare *Zahl*), valley, now only used, for historical reasons, in some German names; e. g.: —

Günt(h)er, *Lothar*, *Lothringen*, Lorraine, *Mathilde*, Matilda, *Walt(h)er*, Walter.

th = [t] is also written in Greek and other foreign words, e. g. *Theater*, theatre, *T(h)ee*, tea.

---

[1] In other words *z* is written instead of *t* when unaccented *e* follows; e. g. *Grazie*, grace. When preceded by *s*, *t* = [t]; e. g. *Hostie*, host.

tt.

Invariably = [t]; e. g. *fett*, fat, *bitter*, bitter.

tz.

Always = [ts]; e. g. *sitzen*, sit, *Satz*, sentence.

u.

1. = [u:] in open syllables; e. g. *du*, thou, *rufen*, call; and before simple final consonants; e. g. *gut*, good.

Before final *fs* (when not standing for *ss*) = [s] in: —
Fuſs, foot, *Gruſs*, greeting, *Ruſs*, soot.

Before *ch* (which does not stand for *chch*) = [x] in: —
Bruch, fen,[1] *Buch*, book, *Buche*, beech, *Fluch*, curse, *Kuchen*, cake, *ruchbar*, notorious, *suchen*, seek, *Tuch*, cloth, *Wucher*, usury.

Often before *chs* = [ks] in
Wuchs, growth, *wuchs*, grew,
and before *sch* = [ʃ] in *wusch*, washed.

EXCEPTIONS. — Short [ʊ] before simple consonant, including *th*, in: —
Klub,[2] club, *plus*, plus, *Luther* (name), *Rum*, rum, *um*, round, about, *Ur-*, in *Urteil*, verdict, *zum* = *zu dem*, to the, *zur* = *zu der*, to the,

---

[1] Not in *Bruch*, break, rupture.
[2] Pronounced in the German way, = [klʊp].

and unaccented in loan-words; e. g. *Modus*, mode, *Sirup*, syrup.

2. = [u] in closed syllables; e. g. *Mutter*, mother, *Kunst*, art.

EXCEPTIONS. — Long [u:] in closed syllable in: —

Geburt,[1] birth, *Husten*, cough, *Ludwig*, Lewis, *pusten*, pant, *Schuster*, shoemaker, *Wust*, chaos, trash.

3. = [y:] in open syllables, in French loan-words; e. g. *Aperçu*, sketch.

4. = [ʏ] in closed syllables, in French loan-words; e. g. *Budget*, budget.

5. = [v] in the combination *qu*. See *qu*.

uh.

Invariably = [u:]; e. g. *Kuh*, cow.

ui.

Pronounced [uɪ] in *hui*, ho, *pfui*, fie.

um, un.

Pronounced [œ̃:] in French words such as *Parfum*, perfume, *Vingt-un*.[2]

ü.

1. = [y:], in open syllables; e. g. *müde*,

---

[1] Rarely pronounced [u]; but always short [ʏ] in *gebürtig*, native.

[2] North German pronunciation, [œŋ].

tired; and before simple final consonants; e. g. *für*, for.

Before *fs* = [s] in *süfs*, sweet.
Before *sch* = [ʃ] in *Rüsche*, ruche.

2. = [ʏ] in closed syllables; e. g. *Hütte*, hut, *Bürde*, burden.

EXCEPTIONS. — Long [y:] in closed syllable in: —

düster, gloomy, *Nüster*, nostril, *Rüster*, elm. *wüst*, waste.

üh.

Invariably = [y:]; e. g. *kühn*, bold.

v.

1. = [f] in German words; e. g. *viel*, much; also in the old loan-words
Veilchen (*Veiel*), violet, *Veit*, Vitus, Guy, *Vers*, verse, *Vogt*, governor;
and always when final; e. g. *Motiv*, motive.

2. = [v] in foreign words, mostly of Latin or Romance origin; e. g. *Vase*, vase, *oval*, oval.

w.

Regularly pronounced [v]; e. g. *wohl*, well.
For *ow* = [o:] see *ow*.

x.

1. Regularly pronounced [ks]; e. g. *Axt*, axe, *Index*, index.

THE LETTERS OF THE ALPHABET.

2. = [ʃ] in *Don Quixote*[1] (name).
3. Mute in French forms such as *Bureaux*,[2] offices.

Y.

1. = [y:], rather than [i:], in open syllables; e. g. *Mythe*, myth; and before simple final consonants; e. g. *Asyl*, refuge.
2. = [Y], rather than [I], in closed syllables; e. g. *Myrte*, myrtle.
    Also in unaccented *yr*, as in *Satyr*, satyr, etc.
3. = [i:] in names, e. g. *Schwyz*.
4. = [I] in names, e. g. *Hyrtl*.
5. = [j], initial or medial; e. g. *loyal*, loyal.

Z.

1. Regularly = [ts]; e. g. *zu*, to, too.
2. = [z] in a few foreign words; e. g.: — *Gaze*, gauze, *Vezier* (= *Wesir*), vizier.[3]

ZZ.

Pronounced [ts] in Italian loan-words; e. g. — *Skizze*, sketch, *Strazze*, rough note book.

---

[1] = [dɔ̃:kıʃɔt] — North German pronunciation, [dɔŋkıʃɔt] —, as if spelt in the French way, *Don Quichotte*. Rarely = [dɔnki'xo:tə].

[2] But *Bureaus*, which is also used, = [by'ro:s].

[3] *Bronze*, bronze, is generally pronounced [brõ:sə]; North German, [brɔŋsə].

GERMAN ACCENT,
AND OTHER PECULIARITIES OF GERMAN PRONUNCIATION.

It has often been remarked that a person may speak a language with perfect correctness and fluency, and yet be detected as a foreigner, because he has not yet acquired the native *accent*.

It will usually be found, however, that, although grammar and idiom may be faultless, yet either the general mode of articulation or the laws of sound peculiar to the language have been imperfectly mastered. Apart from these points, what is commonly called accent still comprises two very different things, viz. *stress,* and *pitch* or *tone*.

MODE OF ARTICULATION.

The German mode of articulation, as differing from the English, may be said to be characterized by the formation of the vowels, especially the round vowels, and of the dentals, as described above (see chapter on German Sounds), the tongue-articulation being more forward and determined, and the lips freely used in the formation both of vowel and consonant-sounds. To German ears, spoken English, as well as German pronounced in the English way, sounds to a certain degree unarticulated.

LAWS OF SOUND.

Of German sound-laws (which mainly result from the peculiarities of German articulation and accentuation), the following are the most important for English speakers. Several have previously been alluded to.

1. Initial vowels, unless almost unaccented and closely connected with the preceding word, are preceded by the glottal stop, [?], even when occurring in the interior of compound words; e. g. *all* [?al], *überall* [?y:bər'?al], everywhere.

2. Final vowels, except unaccented *e* = [ə], and the vowel *a* in the interjections *da* [da], there, *na* [na], well, etc., are long, whether primarily accented or not; e. g. *du* [du:], thou, *Kakadu* [kakadu:], cockatoo.

3. Long vowels are strictly simple vowels, and not diphthongal as English *oo* = [u:w] in *fool*, etc. (see examples under 2).

4. Final consonants, except liquids (*l, m, n, ng, r*), are voiceless and sharp, even when spelt *b, d, g*; e. g. *ab* [?ap], off, *Sieg* [zi:ᵏ/ᵩ], victory.

5. Final consonants, liquids included, are short, even after short vowels; e. g. *Quell* [kvɛl] well, *Hand* [hant], hand.

6. Long consonants only occur instead of double consonants, either in composition, or where two words are closely connected; e. g. *mitteilen* [mɪtːaɪlən], communicate, *not tun* [noːtːuːn], be needful, with long [t], — only when particular distinctness is intended, [noːt tuːn].

In rapid speech, the simple *short* consonant is generally pronounced: [mɪtaɪlən], [noːtuːn].

7. If final voiceless consonants are closely followed by their voiced correspondents, the following vowel not bearing a principal accent, the voiced sound is generally omitted; e. g. *hast du* [hastuː], instead of [hast duː], hast thou, *muſs sich* [musɪç], instead of [mʊs zɪç], must... itself.

8. Initial [z] preceded in composition by a voiceless consonant often becomes [s]; e. g. *Absicht* [ˀapsɪçt], intention, instead of the normal [ˀapzɪçt].

The following changes commonly take place and may be tolerated in fluent conversational German, not, however in public speaking, in reading, etc.

9. [p] in [mp] followed by a third consonant, especially by [f], is often omitted; e. g. *Kampf* [kamf], instead of [kampf], combat.

For initial [pf], simple [f] is frequent; e. g. *Pferd* [feːrt], instead of [pfeːrt], horse.

10. [t] in [nt] followed by a third consonant, especially by [s], is similarly often omitted; e. g. *ganz* [gans], instead of [gants], whole.

11. [ǝn] often becomes either [n]; or else, in rather slovenly speech, [m] after labials, [n] after dentals, [ŋ] after gutturals (see pages 30 seq.).

STRESS AND EMPHASIS.
STRESS.

As in English, the different syllables of words of more than one syllable are pronounced with different degrees of force. As the accentuation is in most cases correctly indicated in dictionaries, and partly in grammars in ordinary use, it will here be sufficient to point out the leading principles.

SIMPLE WORDS.
Genuine German Words.

In genuine German words, the radical syllable, which is also the first syllable of the word, has the principal accent or *stress*, the remaining syllables weaker stresses,[1] only prefixes and suffixes with *e* = [ǝ] being altogether unaccented; e. g. EIn, one, EIne, one (fem.), EInig, at one,

---

[1] Only the principal stress is marked in the following examples.

Einigen, unite, Einigung, agreement, VerEin, association, geEinigt, united, VerEinigung, union, etc.

EXCEPTIONS: ForElle, trout, lebEndig, alive; mostly also luthErisch, Lutheran.[1]

German words with terminations of foreign origin which are regularly accented, are not really exceptions. Such endings are: ei, e. g. BettelEI, beggary; ieren, e. g. hausIEren, peddle; ur, e. g. GlasUR, glazing; enser, ensisch, e. g. BadEnser, inhabitant of Baden, badEnsisch, belonging to Baden (cp. AtheniEnser, atheniEnsisch, Athenian, etc.).

Loan-Words.

Loan-words, except those which have become perfectly naturalized, as a rule retain their original accent.

Such loan-words as were incorporated into the language in the Old High German period (before 1100 A. D.) are no longer foreign in form, and are accented in the German way. They are mostly of Latin origin. E. g. MÜnze, mint, FEnster, window. — Unsettled (in sing.): Altar, AltAr, altar.

In the Middle High German period (down to about 1500 A. D.) many French words found

---

[1] In lebEndig, the stress has been shifted to the following heavy syllable; ForElle and luthErisch may have been influenced by loan-words such as KapElle, chapel, äthErisch, ethereal.

their way into German. They have partly submitted to German accentuation, and are quite German in appearance, e. g. A*benteuer*, adventure, *Dutzend*, dozen; partly the French stress is preserved, e. g. *PartEI*, party, *turnIEren*, joust. — Doublets: *BAnner* — *PanIEr*, banner, *DEmant* — *DiamAnt*, diamond.

Words received into the language in the Modern High German period mostly retain their foreign accent, as also other traces of their foreign origin; e. g. *adiEU*, good-bye, *HotEl*, hotel. — Latin-French doublets with regard to stress: *Phänomen*, *PhänomEn* [-'me:n], phenomenon, etc.

Of words in *ik*, some follow the Latin accentuation, others the French. To the latter class (with stress on *ik*) belong: — *FabrIk*, works, *KatholIk*, catholic, *KritIk*, critique, *PolitIk*, politics, *RepublIk*, republic, *publIk*, public, and mostly also: — *ArithmetIk*, arithmetic, *MathematIk*, mathematics, *MusIk*, music, *PhysIk*, physics.[1]

On words in *ie* see pages 81 seqq.

Words in *or* are mostly taken from the Latin and accentuated accordingly; e. g. *Autor*, author, *Doktor*, doctor, etc., the stress shifting to the termination in the plural; e. g. *Autoren*, with *o* = [o:].[2] So also *Dämon*, demon, plur. *Dämonen*.

---

[1] But Latin accent in *Kritiker*, critic, *Politiker*, politician, *MathemAtiker*, mathematician, etc.

[2] Stress on *or* = [o:r] also in the sing. e. g. in *Humor*, humor, *Meteor*, meteor, *Tenor*, tenor voice.

There is similar shifting of stress in Äther, ether — äthErisch, etherial, BAlsam, balsam, balm — balsAmisch, balsamic, etc.

In words of like termination that are frequently used in juxtaposition the stress is often drawn back on the first syllable, e. g. Nominativ, nominative, GEnitiv, genitive, etc.

Of names accented on the final syllables, besides AthEn, Athens, FlorEnz, Florence, Korinth, Corinth, Paris, Turin, may be mentioned: MerAn, Tirol, and North German (originally Slavonic) names of towns in in, e. g. Berlin, Stettin. Observe German stress in Koblenz, Coblence, Konstanz, Constance.

COMPOUNDS.
General Remarks.

1. In compounds the first part of which is a nominal stem, the radical syllable of the first component (this being in most cases the individualizing part of the whole word) as a rule bears the principal stress, the radical syllables of the remaining components weaker stresses (>); e. g. HAusherr, master of the house, HAusherrnwürde, the dignity of being the master of the house.

If, however, the last component is the individualizing one, it in its turn receives the stress (<); e. g. Jahrhundert, century; but again, e. g. PEstjahrhundert, century of the plague.

Equal stress (=), as in English *steel-pen*, *twenty-one*, only rarely occurs in German, and mostly serves to emphasize the meaning of the second part of the compound; e. g. st*E*inr*E*ich, enormously rich.

2. It is necessary to distinguish between independent compounds, and compounds derived from such. E. g. in *Übertr*E*ibung*, exaggeration, the stress is on the second part, because the word is not compounded of *über*, over, and "*Treibung*" (as, e. g. *Übermafs*, excess, is of *über*, and *Mafs*, measure), but derived from the verb *übertr*E*iben*, exaggerate.

3. The prefixes *be*, *emp*, *ent*, *er*, *ge*, *ver*, *zer* are unaccented, unless the accent be shifted on to them for the sake of contradistinction; e. g. v*E*rgehen, perish — *z*E*rgehen*, dissolve.

Special Remarks.

I. Nouns.

1. The *second* part of the compound, instead of the first, is accented: —

(a) In loose compounds consisting of adjective and noun; e. g. (*der*) *Hohepr*I*Ester*, high-priest.

(b) In most compound geographical names the first part of which is an adjective or a genitive case; e. g. *Langens*A*lza, Königsw*I*nter*.[1]

---

[1] Names in *born, bronn, brück, brunn, förde, grätz, hall, münde, reuth, rode, walde, werth, wörth* regularly

(c) In compounds denoting a period of time, the first part being a genitive case; e. g. *Tages-anfang*, beginning of the day. So also *Jahrhundert*, century, and similar terms.

(d) In compound names of holy days; e. g. *Palmsonntag*, Palm Sunday.

(e) In some compounds, the second part of which is itself a compound, as long as, or longer than the first; e. g. *Generalpostmeister*, postmaster general.

(f) Sometimes in *Neujahr*, New Year, *Bürgermeister*, mayor.

2. Both parts of the compound have *equal stress*: —

(a) In double names forming loose compounds, such as *Hessen-Nassau*.

(b) In compounds the first part of which only serves to emphasize, not exactly to qualify,

---

have this accentuation; e. g. *Paderborn*, *Heilbronn*, *Osnabrück*, *Reinhardsbrunn*, *Eckernförde*, *Königgrätz*, *Reichenhall*, *Swinemünde*, *Gailenreuth*, *Eberswalde*, *Kaiserswerth*, *Donauwörth*. Other names, however, in spite of their being compounded with an adjective or genitive case, are treated like simple words; e. g. *Oberndorf*; *Karlsbad*, *Karlsruhe*, *Landshut*. So also *Greifswald* in the correct local pronunciation; but like *Stralsund*, it is frequently mispronounced with stress on the second (the latter e. g. in Schiller's *Wallenstein*). Observe the German pronunciation of *Hannover*, Hanover, with stress on *o*, the word being originally a compound (= *hohen Ufer*, high bank). -- Again: *Elberfeld*.

the meaning of the second; e. g. Er*sch*Elm, arch rogue.[1]

(c) In long compounds both parts of which are again compounded; e. g. *Vordergaumen*REIbe*laut*, palatal continuant.

3. Shifting of stress pretty frequently occurs when the first portion is itself compounded and the second word of it might possibly form the first word of the second portion; e. g. *Landgerichtsdirektor*, as if compounded of *L*And and *Gerichtsdirektor*, although really = *L*And*gerichts* + *Dir*Ektor.

II. Adjectives and Adverbs.

1. The *second*, instead of the first part, bears the principal stress: —

(a) In *leib*EIgen, held in thraldom, *herz*EIgen, most beloved, *voll*kommen, perfect, *will*kommen, welcome, where the first part is no longer felt as qualifying the second.

(b) In the adjective *ausgez*EIchnet, excellent, as distinct from the p. p. AUs*gezeichnet*. So also mostly *fortw*ährend (adj. and adv.), continual(ly), *ausn*Ehmend (adv.), uncommonly.

(c) In compounds the first part of which is *all*, only serving to generalize or emphasize the

---

[1] But *Judas der* Erz*schelm* (= miscreant), just as E*r*z*bischof*, archbishop; etc.

meaning of the word; e. g. *allgemEIn*, general: so also in compounds with *hoch*; e. g. *hochwÜrdig*, reverend.

(*d*) In compounds the first part of which forms an attribute of a following substantive stem; e. g. *hohepriEsterlich*, pontifical.

(*e*) In loose compounds such as *menschenmÖglich*, within the power of man.

(*f*) In some adjectives in *lich*: —
abschEulich, abominable, *absOnderlich*, particular, *augenblIcklich*, instantaneous, *augenschEInlich*, evident, *ausdrÜcklich*, express, *ausfÜhrlich*, detailed, *aufserordentlich*, extraordinary, *eigentÜmlich*, peculiar, *handgrEIflich*, obvious, *hauptsÄchlich*, principal, *ursprÜnglich*, original, *vornEhmlich*, especial(ly), *vortrEfflich*, excellent, *vorzÜglich*, exquisite, *wahrschEInlich*, probable; often also in *absIchtlich*, intentional.

(*g*) In some adjectives in *ig*: — *barmhErzig*, merciful, *dreiEInig*, *dreifAltig*, triune, *herzInnig*, heartfelt; mostly in *wahrhAftig*, true (always when adv.), *zukÜnftig*, future; often in *armsElig*, miserable, *aufrIchtig*, sincere, *freiwIllig*, voluntary, *holdsElig*, most lovely, *inbrÜnstig*, ardent, *notwEndig*, necessary.

(*h*) Mostly in *offenbAr*, manifest.

(*i*) In compounds with *alt*, such as *altEnglisch*, Old English, *altnordisch*, Old Norse, Icelandic, etc., because they are often used in juxtaposition.[1]

(k) In compounds with *un*, if the second part of the compound is a verbal adjective,—the radical syllable of the verb bearing the stress; e. g. *unerhörbar*, inaudible, *unabänderlich*, unalterable;[2] if the second part is a p. p. with accented prefix, the latter retains the accent; e. g. *unangemeldet*, not announced.— Other adjectives, not derived from verbs: *ungeheuer*, immense (but subst. = U*ngeheuer*, monster), *ungemein*, uncommon.

2. Both parts of the compound have *equal stress*: —

(a) In compounds the first part of which only serves to emphasize the second; e. g. *erzdumm*, very stupid, brainless, *blutarm*, very poor, penniless;[3] etc.

(b) In very long compounds such as *unwiederbringlich*, irrecoverable, instead of *unwiederbringlich* (cf. 1. *k*).

III. Verbs.

1. The *second* part of the compound is accented : —

---

[1] Mostly however *altdeutsch*, *althochdeutsch*, as opposed to *neu(hoch)deutsch*; so also *altfränkisch* = *altmodisch*, old-fashioned.

[2] So also *unmöglich*, impossible; *möglich* being derived from *mögen* (= *vermögen*), to be able.

[3] But *blutarm*, anemic, with stress on the first part.

(a) In compounds the first part of which is the inseparable prefix *mifs*; e. g. *mifsbrAUchen*, abuse.
(b) In compounds with the inseparable prefix *voll*; e. g. *vollEnden*, complete (not where *voll* is a separable adjective, as in *vollgiefsen*, to fill to the brim).
(c) In compounds with the inseparable prefixes *durch, hinter, über, um, unter, wieder*; e. g. *durchdrıngen*, permeate, fill, *hinterbrıngen*, communicate (secretly), *übersEtzen*, translate, *umzıEhen*, enclose, *unterstEllen*, presuppose, *wiederholen*, repeat (not where *durch, hinter*, etc., are separable adverbs = *hindurch, dahinter*, etc.; as *dvrchdringen*, force one's way through; etc.).

IV. Particles.

Compound particles as a rule are accented not on the first, but on the *second* part; e. g. *bergAUf*, up hill, *alsbAld*, forthwith.

The following words are, however, accented on the *first* part: — *Also*, consequently, *dEnnoch*, nevertheless, *wIEderum*, again, which are no longer looked upon as compounds; so also frequently *vorher*, before, *nAchher*, afterwards, *grAdaus*, straight on, *bEInah*, *bEInahe*, almost, *AUfserdem*, besides, *trotzdem*, nevertheless; *AUfserhalb*, outside, *oberhalb*, above, etc.; *EInerlei*, of one kind (but *einerlEI*, no matter), *zwEIerlei*, of two kinds, different, *dErlei*, of that kind, etc.; *EInmal*, once, a single time (but *einmAl*, once = some time), *zwEImal*, twice, etc.;[1] *dAmals*, then, *nIEmals*, never, etc.; *hInterrücks*, backwards, from behind; *dIEsseits*, on this side, *jEnseits*, on the other side; *Aufwärts*, upward, *vorwärts*, forward; *krEuzweis*, crosswise, *pAArweis*, in pairs, etc.; mostly *dIEsfalls*, in that case, *glEIchfalls*, likewise, etc.; *fErnerhin*, for the future, etc.; *mEInetwegen*, *mEInethalben*, on my account, for aught I care, etc.; *mEInesteils*, for my part, etc.

EMPHASIS.

Sentence-stress, or *emphasis*, is, as the word-stress, on the whole logical in German, the most important word bearing the strongest accent, whilst other words receive weaker stresses, or are comparatively unaccented. The predicate or, if there is any, the object being as a rule the individualizing word in the sentence, the predicate or the object is generally the accented word; e. g. *ich schrEIbe*, I write, *der Hund bEllt*, the dog barks, *er ist krAnk*, he is ill, *ich schreibe einen BrIEf*, I write a letter. Attributive adjectives in most cases have a somewhat weaker stress than the word which they qualify, e. g. *die kindliche LIEbe*, filial love; but *des KIndes*

---

[1] If used emphatically, often with level stress: — *vorhEr*, *nAchhEr*, *grAdAus*, etc.; *EInmAl*, *zwEImAl*, etc.

Liebe, die Liebe des Kindes, die Liebe zu dem Kinde. —

In English, sentence-stress is very similar. English speakers of German, however, are inclined to accent too strongly the verbal forms following the object, in such clauses as *einen Brief schreiben,* to write a letter, *einen Brief geschrieben haben,* to have written a letter, *wenn ich einen Brief schreibe,* when I writte a letter.

TONE (PITCH).[1]

All voice-sounds used in speech (vowels and voiced consonants) must have a certain pitch, and may, therefore, also be considered as tones. In speaking, the voice only rarely dwells on one note, but is constantly gliding upwards or downwards. There are three simple, or primary, inflections of tone: level (—), rising (/), and falling (\). Rise and fall can be varied indefinitely according to the interval through which they pass.

Relations of tone have as yet been only imperfectly studied, and they probably offer the greatest difficulty in the practical acquisition of a foreign language. In English and German, tones, however, are similar. In either language

---

[1] Compare Sweet, *Handbook of Phonetics*, pages 93 seqq. (corresponding to the same author's *Primer of Phonetics*, 2nd ed., pages 68 seqq.), whence the above more general remarks are mainly drawn.

they are sentence-tones, i. e. they modify the general meaning of the whole sentence, the rising tone being employed in questions and antecedents, the falling tone in answers and statements of facts.

As in Scotch and in American English, peculiarities of inflection, apart from sentence-tone, are met with in provincial German pronunciations, especially in Saxony and on the Lower Rhine. — English speakers must be careful not to place a high tone (a fourth?) on the first of two words with equal stress (*Ehre und Ruhm*), or on words with secondary stress preceding the primarily accented one, e. g. an adjective preceding its substantive (*die kindliche Liebe*), the subject preceding the predicate (*der Hund bellt*), or the predicate preceding the object (*ich schreibe einen Brief*), as is the rule in recitation, especially in pathetic passages, in English.

SPECIMENS.

⁎ In these Specimens o is used for œ (open ö).

Habe nun, ach! Philosophie,
Juristerei und Medizin,
Und, leider! auch Theologie
Durchaus studiert, mit heißem Bemüh'n.
Da steh' ich nun, ich armer Tor!
Und bin so klug, als wie zuvor;
Heiße Magister, heiße Doktor gar,
Und ziehe schon an die zehen Jahr,
Herauf, herab und quer und krumm,
Meine Schüler an der Nase herum —
Und sehe, daß wir nichts wissen können!
Das will mir schier das Herz verbrennen.
Zwar bin ich gescheiter als alle die Laffen,
Doktoren, Magister, Schreiber und Pfaffen;
Mich plagen keine Skrupel noch Zweifel,
Fürchte mich weder vor Hölle noch Teufel —
Dafür ist mir auch alle Freud' entrissen,
Bilde mir nicht ein, was Recht's zu wissen,
Bilde mir nicht ein, ich könnte was lehren,
Die Menschen zu bessern und zu bekehren.
Auch hab' ich weder Gut noch Geld,
Noch Ehr' und Herrlichkeit der Welt;
Es möchte kein Hund so länger leben!
Drum hab' ich mich der Magie ergeben,
Ob mir durch Geistes Kraft und Mund
Nicht manch Geheimnis würde kund,
Daß ich nicht mehr, mit saurem Schweiß,
Zu sagen brauche, was ich nicht weiß,

Proben.

(Langsam abgemessener Vortrag.)
haːbə nuːn, 'ʔax! fiːloˑzoˑ'fiː,
juːrɪstə'rai ʔunt meːdiˑ'tsiːn,
ʔunt, 'laidər! ʔaux teːoˑloˑ'giː
durç'ʔaus ʃtuˑ'diːrt, mɪt 'haisəm bə'myːn.
daː 'ʃteː ʔɪç[1] nuːn, ʔɪç 'ʔarmər ″toːr!
ʔunt bɪn zoː 'kluːk, ʔals viː tsuː'foːr;
haisə ma'gɪstər, haisə ″dɔktɔr gaːr,
ʔunt 'tsiːə ʃoːn ʔan diː 'tseːən 'jaːr,
hɛ'rauf, hɛ'rap ʔunt 'kveːr ʔunt 'krum,
mainə 'ʃyːlər ʔan dɛr 'naːzə hɛrum —
ʔunt 'zeːə, das viːr 'nɪçts ″vɪsən kənən!
das vɪl miːr ʃiːr das 'hɛrts fɛr'brɛnən.
tsvaːr bɪn ʔɪç gə'ʃaitər ʔals 'ʔalə diː 'lafən,
dɔk'toːrən, ma'gɪstər, 'ʃraibər ʔunt 'pfafən,
mɪç 'plaːgən kainə 'skruːpəl nɔx 'tsvaifəl,
'fyrçtə mɪç veːdər foːr 'hələ nɔx 'tɔyfəl —
daːfyːr ʔɪst miːr ʔaux 'ʔalə ″frɔyt ʔɛnt'rɪsən,
bɪldə miːr nɪçt 'ʔain, vas 'rɛçts tsuː ″vɪsən,
bɪldə miːr nɪçt 'ʔain, ʔɪç kəntə vas ″leːrən,
diː 'mɛnʃən tsuː ″besərn ʔunt tsuː bə″keːrən.
ʔaux haːp ʔɪç[2] veːdər 'guːt nɔx 'gɛlt,
nɔx 'ʔeːr ʔunt 'hɛrlɪçkait dɛr 'vɛlt;
ʔɛs mɛçtə kain ″hunt 'zoː 'lɛŋər 'leːbən!
drum haːp ʔɪç[2] mɪç dɛr ma'giː ʔɛrgeːbən,
ʔɔp miːr durç ″gaistəs 'kraft ʔunt 'munt
nɪçt manç gə'haimnɪs vyrdə 'kunt,
das ʔɪç nɪçt 'meːr, mɪt zaurəm 'ʃvais,
tsuː 'zaːgən brauxə, vas ʔɪç nɪçt 'vais,

---

[1] Oder: [ʃteɪ-ɪç].   [2] [haːb-ɪç].

Daß ich erkenne, was die Welt
Im Innersten zusammenhält,
Schau' alle Wirkenskraft und Samen,
Und tu' nicht mehr in Worten kramen.
  O sähst du, voller Mondenschein,
Zum letztenmal auf meine Pein,
Den ich so manche Mitternacht
An diesem Pult herangewacht:
Dann, über Büchern und Papier,
Trübsel'ger Freund, erschienst du mir!
Ach! könnt' ich doch auf Bergeshöh'n
In deinem lieben Lichte gehn,
Um Bergeshöhle mit Geistern schweben,
Auf Wiesen in deinem Dämmer weben,
Von allem Wissensqualm entladen,
In deinem Tau gesund mich baden!
                        GOETHE, *Faust*.

Durch diese hohle Gasse muß er kommen;
Es führt kein andrer Weg nach Küßnacht — hier
Vollend' ich's — die Gelegenheit ist günstig.
Dort der Holunderstrauch verbirgt mich ihm;
Von dort herab kann ihn mein Pfeil erlangen;
Des Weges Enge wehret den Verfolgern.
Mach deine Rechnung mit dem Himmel, Vogt!
Fort mußt du, deine Uhr ist abgelaufen.
  Ich lebte still und harmlos — das Geschoß
War auf das Waldes Tiere nur gerichtet,

das ʔɪç ʔɛr'kɛnə, vas diː 'vɛlt
ʔɪm 'ʔɪnərstən tsuː'zamənhɛlt,
'ʃau 'ʔalə 'vɪrkənskraft ʔʊnt 'zaːmən,
ʔʊnt tuː nɪçt meːr ʔɪn 'vɔrtən kraːmən.

'ʔoː 'zɛːst duː, 'folər 'moːndənʃain,
tsʊm 'lɛtstənmaːl ʔauf mainə 'pain,
deːn ʔɪç zoː 'mançə 'mɪtərnaxt
ʔan diːzəm 'pʊlt hɛ'ranɡəvaxt:
'dan, ʔyːbər 'byːçərn ʔʊnt pa·'piːr,
'tryːpzeːlgər[1] 'frɔynt, ʔɛr'ʃiːnst duː miːr!
'ʔax! kɔnt ʔɪç dɔx ʔauf 'bɛrɡəsheːn
ʔɪn dainəm 'liːbən 'lɪçtə ɡeːn,
ʔʊm 'bɛrɡəsheːlə mɪt 'ɡaistərn ʃveːbən,
ʔauf 'viːzən ʔɪn dainəm 'dɛmər veːbən,
fɔn 'ʔaləm 'vɪsənskvalm ʔɛnt'laːdən,
ʔɪn dainəm 'tau ɡə"zʊnt mɪç baːdən!
'ɡøːtə, 'faust.

(Langsamer Vortrag.)
dʊrç 'diːzə 'hoːlə 'ɡasə 'mʊs ʔeːr 'komən;
ʔɛs fyːrt kain 'ʔandrər 'veːk naːx 'kysnaxt — 'hiːr
fɔ'lɛnt ʔɪçs[2] — diː ɡə'leːɡənhait ʔɪst 'ɡynstɪç.
'dɔrt dɛr ho'lʊndərʃtraux fɛr'bɪrkt mɪç ʔiːm;
fɔn 'dɔrt hɛ'rap kan ʔiːn main 'pfail ʔɛr'laŋən;
dɛs 'veːɡəs 'ʔɛŋə 'veːrət dɛn fɛr'fɔlgərn.
max dainə 'rɛçnʊŋ mɪt dɛm 'hɪməl, 'foːkt!
'fɔrt 'mʊst duː, dainə 'ʔuːr ʔɪst 'ʔapɡəlaufən.

ʔɪç 'leːptə 'ʃtɪl ʔʊnt 'harmloːs — das ɡə'ʃɔs
vaːr ʔauf dɛs 'valdəs 'tiːrə nuːr ɡərɪçtət,

[1] Bühnenaussprache: [-jər]. [2] Oder: [fɔ'lɛnd-ɪçs].

Meine Gedanken waren rein von Mord —
Du hast aus meinem Frieden mich heraus
Geschreckt; in gärend Drachengift hast du
Die Milch der frommen Denkart mir verwandelt;
Zum Ungeheuren hast du mich gewöhnt —
Wer sich des Kindes Haupt zum Ziele setzte,
Der kann auch treffen in das Herz des Feinds.
. . . .
Auf dieser Bank von Stein will ich mich setzen,
Dem Wanderer zur kurzen Ruh' bereitet —
Denn hier ist keine Heimat — jeder treibt
Sich an dem andern rasch und fremd vorüber
Und fraget nicht nach seinem Schmerz — hier geht
Der sorgenvolle Kaufmann und der leicht
Geschürzte Pilger — der andächt'ge Mönch,
Der düstre Räuber und der heitre Spielmann,
Der Säumer mit dem schwer beladenen Roß,
Der ferne herkommt von der Menschen Ländern —
Denn jede Straße führt ans End' der Welt —
Sie alle ziehen ihres Weges fort
An ihr Geschäft — und meines ist der Mord!
    SCHILLER, *Wilhelm Tell*.

Römer! Mitbürger! Freunde! Hört mich meine
Sache führen; und seid still, damit ihr hören möget.
Glaubt mir um meiner Ehre willen, und hegt
Achtung vor meiner Ehre, damit ihr glauben mögt.
Richtet mich nach eurer Weisheit, und weckt eure

maine gə'daŋkən vaːrən 'rain fɔn 'mɔrt —
'duː hast ʔaus mainəm 'friːdən mɪç heˈraus
gəʃrɛkt; ʔɪn 'gɛːrənt 'draxəngɪft hast duː
diː 'mɪlç der 'frɔmən 'dɛŋkʔaːrt miːr ferˈvandəlt;
tsʊm ʔʊŋgəˈhɔyrən hast duː mɪç gəˈvɛːnt —
veːr zɪç dɛs ˮkɪndəs 'haupt tsʊm 'tsiːlə zɛtstə,
deːr kan ʔaux 'trɛfən ʔɪn das 'hɛrts dɛs ˮfaints.

. . . .

ʔauf diːzər 'baŋk fɔn 'ʃtain vɪl ʔɪç mɪç 'zɛtsən,
deːm 'vandərər tsʊr 'kʊrtsən 'ruː bəraitət —
dɛn hiːr ʔɪst 'kainə ˮhaimaːt — 'jeːdər traipt
zɪç ʔan dɛm 'ʔandərn 'raʃ ʔʊnt 'frɛmt foːˈryːbər
ʔʊnt 'fraːgət nɪçt naːx zainəm 'ʃmɛrts — hiːr geːt
dɛr zɔrgənfɔlə ˮkaufman ʔʊnt dɛr 'laiçt
gəˈʃʏrtstə ˮpɪlgər — dɛr 'ʔandɛçtgə[1] 'mɵnç,
dɛr 'dyːstrə ˮrɔybər 'ʊnt dɛr 'haitrə ˮʃpiːlman,
dɛr ˮzɔymər mɪt dɛm 'ʃveːr bəˈlaːdnən 'rɔs,
deːr 'fɛrnə 'heːrkɔmt fɔn dɛr 'mɛnʃən 'lɛndərn —
dɛn 'jeːdə 'ʃtraːsə fyːrt ʔans 'ʔɛnt dɛr 'vɛlt —
ziː 'ʔalə 'tsiːən ʔiːrəs 'veːgəs fɔrt
ʔan ʔiːr gəˈʃɛft — ʔʊnt 'mainəs ʔɪst dɛr ˮmɔrt!
ˮʃɪlər, 'vɪlhɛlm ˮtɛl.

(Langsamer Vortrag.)
'reːmər! ˮmɪtbʏrgər! ˮ'frɔyndə! 'hɛːrt mɪç mainə
'zaxə fyːrən; ʔʊnt zait 'ʃtɪl, daːˈmɪt ʔiːr 'heːrən meːgət.
'glaupt miːr ʔʊm mainər 'ʔeːrə vɪlən, ʔʊnt heːkt
'ʔaxtʊŋ foːr mainər ʔeːrə, daːˈmɪt ʔiːr 'glaubən meːkt.
'rɪçtət mɪç naːx ʔɔyrər 'vaishait, ʔʊnt 'vɛkt ʔɔyrə

---
[1] Bühnenaussprache: [-jə].

Sinne, um desto besser urteilen zu können. Ist jemand in dieser Versammlung, irgend ein herzlicher Freund Cäsars, dem sage ich: des Brutus Liebe zum Cäsar war nicht geringer als seine. Wenn dieser Freund dann fragt, warum Brutus gegen Cäsar aufstand, ist dies meine Antwort: nicht, weil ich Cäsarn weniger liebte, sondern weil ich Rom mehr liebte. Wolltet ihr lieber, Cäsar lebte und ihr stürbet alle als Sklaven, als daß Cäsar tot ist, damit ihr alle lebet wie freie Männer? Weil Cäsar mich liebte, wein' ich um ihn; weil er glücklich war, freue ich mich; weil er tapfer war, ehr' ich ihn, aber weil er herrschsüchtig war, erschlug ich ihn. Also Tränen für seine Liebe, Freude für sein Glück, Ehre für seine Tapferkeit, und Tod für seine Herrschsucht. Wer ist hier so niedrig gesinnt, daß er ein Knecht sein möchte? Ist es jemand, er rede, denn ihn habe ich beleidigt. Wer ist hier so roh, daß er nicht wünschte, ein Römer zu sein? Ist es jemand, er rede, denn ihn habe ich beleidigt. Ich halte inne, um Antwort zu hören.

SHAKESPEARE, *Julius Cäsar*,
übersetzt von A. W. v. SCHLEGEL.

Wohltätig ist des Feuers Macht,
Wenn sie der Mensch bezähmt, bewacht,
Und was er bildet, was er schafft,
Das dankt er dieser Himmelskraft;
Doch furchtbar wird die Himmelskraft,

'zīnə, ʔum dɛsto: 'bɛsər 'ʔurtailən tsu˙ kənən. 'ʔɪst 'jeː-
mant ʔɪn diːzər fɛr'zamluŋ, 'ʔɪrgənt ʔain 'hɛrtslɪçər
"froynt"tsɛːzars,'deːm'zaːgəʔɪç:dɛs"bruːtʊs'liːbə tsʊm
'tsɛːzar vaːr nɪçt gə'rɪŋər ʔals "zainə. vɛn diːzər
'froynt dan 'fraːkt, vaː'rʊm 'bruːtʊs geːgən 'tsɛːzar
"ʔaufʃtant, ʔɪst 'diːs mainə 'ʔantvɔrt: 'nɪçt, vail ʔɪç
'tsɛːzarn "veːnɪgər liːptə, zɔndərn vail ʔɪç 'roːm "meːr
liːptə. vɔltət ʔiːr 'liːbər,'tsɛːzar"leːptə ʔunt 'ʔiːr ʃtʏrbət
'ʔalə ʔals"sklaːvən, ʔalsdas'tsɛːzar"toːt ʔɪst,daːmɪt'ʔiːr
'ʔalə "leːbət viː 'fraiə "mɛnər? vail'tsɛːzar mɪç 'liːptə,
'vain ʔɪç¹ ʔʊm ʔiːn; vail ʔeːr 'glʏklɪç vaːr, 'froyə ʔɪç
mɪç; vail ʔeːr'tapfər vaːr,'ʔeːr ʔɪç² ʔiːn, ʔaːbər vail ʔeːr
"hɛrʃzʏçtɪç vaːr, ʔɛr"ʃluːk ʔɪç ʔiːn. ʔalzoː 'treːnən
fyːr zainə 'liːbə, 'froydə fyːr zain 'glʏk, 'ʔeːrə fyːr
zainə 'tapfərkait, ʔunt "toːt fyːr zainə "hɛrʃzʊxt.
veːr ʔɪst hiːr zoː 'niːdrɪç gəzɪnt, das ʔeːr ʔain 'knɛçt
zain məçtə? 'ʔɪst ʔɛs jeːmant, ʔeːr 'reːdə, dɛn 'ʔiːn
haːbə ʔɪç bə'laidɪçt. 'veːr ʔɪst hiːr zoː 'roː, das ʔeːr
nɪçt 'vʏnʃtə, ʔain 'rəːmər tsu˙ zain? 'ʔɪst ʔɛs jeːmant,
ʔeːr 'reːdə, dɛn 'ʔiːn haːbə ʔɪç bə'laidɪçt. ʔɪç haltə
'ʔɪnə, ʔʊm 'ʔantvɔrt tsu˙ həːrən.
        "ʃeːkspiːr, 'juːlɪʊs "tsɛːzar,
ʔyːbər'zɛtst fɔn 'ʔaɪ've: ('ʔaugʊst 'vɪlhɛlm) fɔn "ʃlegəl.

(Im ganzen: langsamer Vortrag.)

"voːltɛːtɪç ʔɪst dɛs "foyərs 'maxt,
vɛn ziː der 'mɛnʃ bə"tsɛːmt, bə"vaxt,
ʔʊnt 'vas ʔeːr 'bɪldət, 'vas ʔeːr 'ʃaft,
das 'daŋkt ʔeːr 'diːzər "hɪməlskraft:
dɔx "fʏrçtbaːr vɪrt di: 'hɪməlskraft,

¹ Oder: ['vain-ɪç]. ² Oder: ['ʔeːr-ɪç].

Wenn sie der Fessel sich entrafft,
Einhertritt auf der eignen Spur,
Die freie Tochter der Natur.
Wehe, wenn sie losgelassen,
Wachsend ohne Widerstand,
Durch die volkbelebten Gassen
Wälzt den ungeheuren Brand!
Denn die Elemente hassen
Das Gebild der Menschenhand.
Aus der Wolke
Quillt der Segen,
Strömt der Regen,
Aus der Wolke, ohne Wahl,
Zuckt der Strahl!
Hört ihr's wimmern hoch vom Turm?
Das ist Sturm!
Rot, wie Blut,
Ist der Himmel,
Das ist nicht des Tages Glut!
Welch Getümmel
Straßen auf!
Dampf wallt auf!
Flackernd steigt die Feuersäule,
Durch der Straße lange Zeile
Wächst es fort mit Windeseile.
Kochend, wie aus Ofens Rachen,
Glühn die Lüfte, Balken krachen,
Pfosten stürzen, Fenster klirren,

Proben.

vɛn ziː dɛr ˈfɛsəl zɪç ʔɛntˈraft,
ʔainˈhɛːrtrɪt ʔauf dɛr ˈʔaignən ˈʃpuːr,
diː ˈfraiə ˈtɔxtər dɛr naːˈtuːr.
ˈveːə, vɛn ziː ˈloːsgəlasən,
ˈvaksənt ʔoːnə ˈviːdərʃtant,
dʊrç diː ˈfɔlkbəleːptən ˈgasən
ˈvɛltst dɛn ʔʊngəˈhɔyrən ˈˈbrant!
dɛn diː ʔeːləˈmɛntə ˈˈhasən
das gəˈbɪlt dɛr ˈmɛnʃənhant.
ʔaus dɛr ˈvɔlkə
ˈkvɪlt dɛr ˈˈzeːgən,
ˈʃtrøːmt dɛr ˈˈreːgən,
ʔaus dɛr ˈvɔlkə, ʔoːnə ˈvaːl,
ˈtsʊkt dɛr ˈˈʃtraːl!
ˈhøːrt ʔiːrs ˈvɪmərn ˈhoːx fɔm ˈtʊrm?
das ʔɪst ˈˈʃtʊrm!
ˈroːt, viː ˈbluːt,
ʔɪst dɛr ˈhɪməl,
das ʔɪst nɪçt dɛs ˈˈtaːgəs ˈgluːt!
vɛlç gəˈtʏməl
ˈʃtraːsən ˈʔauf!
ˈˈdampf ˈvalt ˈʔauf!
ˈflakərnt ˈʃtaikt diː ˈˈfɔyərzɔylə,
dʊrç dɛr ˈʃtraːsə ˈlaŋə ˈtsailə
ˈvɛkst ʔɛs ˈfɔrt mɪt ˈvɪndəsˈʔailə [1].
ˈkɔxənt, viː ʔaus ˈʔoːfəns raxən,
ˈglyːn diː ˈlʏftə, ˈbalkən ˈkraxən,
ˈpfɔstən ˈʃtʏrtsən, ˈfɛnstər ˈklɪrən,

---

[1] Auch: [ˈvɪndəsʔailə].

Kinder jammern, Mütter irren,
Tiere wimmern
Unter Trümmern,
Alles rennet, rettet, flüchtet,
Taghell ist die Nacht gelichtet.
Durch der Hände lange Kette
Um die Wette
Fliegt der Eimer, hoch im Bogen
Spritzen Quellen Wasserwogen.
Heulend kommt der Sturm geflogen,
Der die Flamme brausend sucht.
Prasselnd in die dürre Frucht
Fällt sie, in des Speichers Räume,
In der Sparren dürre Bäume,
Und als wollte sie im Wehen
Mit sich fort der Erde Wucht
Reißen in gewalt'ger Flucht,
Wächst sie in des Himmels Höhen
Riesengroß!
Hoffnungslos
Weicht der Mensch der Götterstärke
Müßig sieht er seine Werke
Und bewundernd untergehen.
    SCHILLER, *Lied von der Glocke.*

 Über allen Gipfeln
 Ist Ruh',
 In allen Wipfeln

'kɪndər 'jamərn, 'mʏtər 'ʔɪrən,
'tiːrə 'vɪmərn
ʔuntər 'trʏmərn,
'ʔaləs 'rɛnət, 'rɛtət, 'flʏçtət,
"taːkhəl ʔɪst diː 'naxt gə'lɪçtət.
durç dɛr 'hɛndə 'laŋə 'kɛtə
ʔum diː 'vɛtə
'fliːkt dɛr 'ʔaimər, 'hoːx ʔɪm 'boːgən
'ʃprɪtsən 'kvɛlən 'vasərvoːgən.
'hɔylənt kɔmt dɛr 'ʃturm gəfloːgən,
deːr diː 'flamə 'brauzənt 'zuːxt.
'prasəlnt ʔɪn diː 'dʏrə 'fruxt
'fɛlt ziː, ʔɪn dɛs 'ʃpaiçərs 'rɔymə,
ʔɪn dɛr 'ʃparən 'dʏrə 'bɔymə,
ʔunt ʔals vɔltə ziː ʔɪm 'veːən
mɪt zɪç 'fɔrt dɛr 'ʔeːrdə 'vuxt
'raisən ʔɪn gə'valtgər[1] 'fluxt,
'vɛkst ziː ʔɪn dɛs 'hɪməls 'høːən
"riːzəngrɔːs!
'hɔfnuŋsloːs
'vaiçt dɛr mɛnʃ dɛr 'gøtərʃtɛrkə,
'myːsɪç ziːt ʔeːr zainə 'vɛrkə
ʔunt bə'vundərnt 'ʔuntərgøːən.
    "ʃɪlər, 'liːt fɔn dɛr "glɔkə.

<hr>

(Langsamer Vortrag.)
ʔyːbər 'ʔalən "gɪpfəln
ʔɪst "ruː;
ʔɪn 'ʔalən "vɪpfəln

<hr>

[1] Bühnenaussprache: [-jər].

Spürest du
Kaum einen Hauch;
Die Vögelein schweigen im Walde.
Warte nur! Balde
Ruhest du auch.

GOETHE.

Du bist wie eine Blume
So hold und schön und rein;
Ich schau dich an, und Wehmut
Schleicht mir ins Herz hinein.

Mir ist, als ob ich die Hände
Aufs Haupt dir legen sollt',
Betend, daß Gott dich erhalte
So rein und schön und hold.

HEINE.

Es ist doch gewiß, daß in der Welt den Menschen nichts notwendig macht als die Liebe. Ich fühl's an Lotten, daß sie mich ungern verlöre, und die Kinder haben keine andre Idee, als daß ich immer morgen wiederkommen würde. Heut war ich hinausgegangen, Lottens Klavier zu stimmen; ich konnte aber nicht dazu kommen, denn die Kleinen verfolgten mich um ein Märchen, und Lotte sagte selbst, ich sollte ihnen den Willen tun. Ich schnitt ihnen das Abendbrot, das sie nun fast so gerne von mir als von Lotten annehmen, und erzählte ihnen das Hauptstückchen von der Prinzessin, die von Händen bedient wird. Ich lerne viel dabei, das versichr' ich dich, und ich bin erstaunt, was

Proben.

'ʃpyːrəst duː
'kaum ʔainən "haux;
diː 'føːgəlain "ʃvaigən ʔɪm valdə.
'vartə nuːr‖ 'baldə
"ruːəst 'duː "ʔaux.   gøːtə.

(Vortrag.)
duː bɪst viː ʔainə "bluːmə
zoː 'hɔlt ʔʊnt 'ʃøːn ʔʊnt 'rain;
ʔɪç ʃau dɪç 'ʔan, ʔʊnt "veːmuːt
ʃlaiçt miːr ʔɪns 'hɛrts hɪnain.
miːr 'ʔɪst, ʔals ʔɔp ʔɪç diː 'hɛndə
ʔaufs 'haupt diːr leːgən zɔlt,
'beːtənt, das 'gɔt dɪç ʔɛr"haltə
zoː "rain ʔʊnt "ʃøːn ʔʊnt "hɔlt.   hainə.

(Gesprächston, größtenteils ruhig erzählend.)
ʔɛs ʔɪst dɔx gə'vɪs, das ʔɪn dər vɛlt dɛn 'mɛnʃən 'nɪçts 'noːtvɛndɪç maxt ʔals diː "liːbə. ʔɪç
fyːls ʔan 'loːtən, das ziː mɪç 'ʔʊngɛrn fɛr'løːrə, ʔʊnt
diː 'kɪndər haːbən kainə 'ʔandrə ʔiː'deː, ʔals das ʔɪç
ʔɪmər 'mɔrgən 'viːdərkɔmən vʏrdə. hɔyt vaːr
ʔɪç hɪ'nausgəgaŋən, 'loːtəns kla'"viːr tsuː ʃtɪmən;
ʔɪç 'kɔntə ʔaːbər nɪçt daːtsuː 'kɔmən, dɛn diː
'klainən fɛrfɔlktən mɪç ʔʊm ʔain "mɛːrçən, ʔʊnt 'loːtə
zaːktə 'zɛlpst, ʔɪç zɔltə ʔiːnən dɛn 'vɪlən tuːn. ʔɪç
'ʃnɪt ʔiːnən das 'ʔaːbəntbroːt, das ziː nuːn 'fast zoː
gɛrnə fɔn 'miːr ʔals fɔn 'loːtən ʔannɛːmən, ʔʊnt fɛr-
'tseːltə ʔiːnən das 'hauptʃtʏkçən fɔn dər prɪn"tsɛsɪn,
diː fɔn "hɛndən bə'diːnt vɪrt. ʔɪç 'lɛrnə 'fiːl daːbai,
das fɛr'zɪçr-ɪç dɪç, ʔʊnt ʔɪç bɪn ʔɛr'ʃtaunt, vas

es auf sie für Eindrücke macht. Weil ich manchmal einen Inzidenzpunkt erfinden muß, den ich beim zweiten Male vergesse, sagen sie gleich, das vorige Mal wär's anders gewest, so daß ich mich jetzt übe, sie unveränderlich in einem singenden Silbenfall an einem Schnürchen weg zu rezitieren. Ich habe daraus gelernt, wie ein Autor durch eine zweite veränderte Auflage seiner Geschichte, und wenn sie noch so poetisch besser geworden wäre, notwendig seinem Buche schaden muß. Der erste Eindruck findet uns willig, und der Mensch ist so gemacht, daß man ihm das Abenteuerlichste überreden kann; das haftet aber auch gleich so fest, und wehe dem, der es wieder auskratzen und austilgen will!

GOETHE, *Die Leiden des jungen Werthers.*

Es zogen drei Bursche wohl über den Rhein,
Bei einer Frau Wirtin, da kehrten sie ein:
„Frau Wirtin! hat sie gut Bier und Wein?
Wo hat sie ihr schönes Töchterlein?"
„Mein Bier und Wein ist frisch und klar.
Mein Töchterlein liegt auf der Totenbahr."
Und als sie traten zur Kammer hinein,
Da lag sie in einem schwarzen Schrein.
Der erste, der schlug den Schleier zurück
Und schaute sie an mit traurigem Blick:
„Ach, lebtest du noch, du schöne Maid!
Ich würde dich lieben von dieser Zeit."

ʔɛs ʔauf ziː fyːr 'ʔaindryḵə maxt. vail ʔɪç mançmaːl
ʔainən ʔmtsiː'dɛntspuŋktʔɛr'fɪndən mus, deːn ʔɪç baim
'tsvaitən maːlə fɛr'gɛsə, 'zaːgən ziː glaiç, das 'foːrɪgə
maːl vɛːrs 'ʔandərs gəveːst, zoː das ʔɪç mɪç jɛtst
'ʔyːbə, ziː ʔunfɛr'ʔɛndərlɪç ʔɪn ʔainəm'zɪŋəndən 'zɪlbən-
fal ʔan 'ʔainəm 'ʃnyːrçən vɛk tsuː reːtsiː'tiːrən. ʔɪç
haːbə daːraus gə'lɛrnt, viː ʔain 'ʔautər durç ʔainə 'tsvaitə
fɛr'ʔɛndərtə 'ʔaufːagə zainər gə'ʃɪçtə, ʔunt vɛn ziː
'nɔx zoː poː'eːtɪʃ 'bɛsər gəvɔrdən vɛːrə, 'noːtvɛndɪç
zainəm buːxə 'ʃaːdən mus. dər 'ʔeːrstə 'ʔaindruk
fɪndət ʔuns 'vɪlɪç, ʔunt dər 'mɛnʃ ʔɪst 'zoː gə'maxt,
das man ʔiːm das 'ʔaːbəntəyərlɪçstə ʔyːbər'reːdən kan:
das 'haftət ʔaːbər ʔaux glaiç 'zoː 'fɛst, ʔunt 'veːə 'deːm,
deːr ʔɛs viːdər 'ʔauskratsən ʔunt 'austɪlgən vɪl!
"geːtə, diː 'laidən dəs 'juŋən "veːrtərs.

(Erzählend; natürlich, aber mit Ausdruck.)

ʔɛs 'tsoːgən drai 'burʃə voːl 'ʔyːbər dən 'rain,
bai ʔainər frau 'vɪrtɪn, daː keːrtən ziː 'ʔain:
„frau 'vɪrtɪn! hat ziː 'guːt 'biːr ʔunt 'vain?
voː hat ziː ʔiːr 'ʃøːnəs "tɛçtərlain?"
„main 'biːr ʔunt 'vain ʔɪst 'frɪʃ ʔunt 'klaːr.
main "tɛçtərlain liːkt ʔauf dər "toːtənbaːr."
ʔunt ʔals ziː traːtən tsur 'kamər hɪnain,
daː 'laːk ziː ʔɪn ʔainəm ʃvartsən 'ʃrain.
der 'ʔeːrstə, deːr ʃluːk dən 'ʃlaiər tsuːryḵ
ʔunt ʃautə ziː 'ʔan mɪt 'trauːrɪgəm 'blɪk:
„'ʔax, 'leːptəst duː nɔx, duː 'ʃøːnə 'mait!
ʔɪç vyrdə dɪç 'liːbən fɔn 'diːzər tsait."

Der zweite deckte den Schleier zu
Und kehrte sich ab und weinte dazu:
„Ach, daß du liegst auf der Totenbahr!
Ich hab' dich geliebet so manches Jahr."
Der dritte hub ihn wieder sogleich
Und küßte sie an den Mund so bleich:
„Dich liebt' ich immer, dich lieb' ich noch heut
Und werde dich lieben in Ewigkeit."

UHLAND.

v. TELLHEIM. Ah! meine Minna! —
DAS FRÄULEIN. Ah! mein Tellheim! —
v. TELLHEIM. Verzeihen Sie, gnädiges Fräulein,
— das Fräulein von Barnhelm hier zu finden —
DAS FRÄULEIN. Kann Ihnen doch so gar unerwartet nicht sein? — Ich soll Ihnen verzeihen, daß ich noch Ihre Minna bin? Verzeih Ihnen der Himmel, daß ich noch das Fräulein von Barnhelm bin! —
v. TELLHEIM. Gnädiges Fräulein —
DAS FRÄULEIN. Mein Herr —
v. TELLHEIM. Wenn wir uns beiderseits nicht irren —
FRANZISKA. Je, Herr Wirt, wen bringen Sie uns denn da? Geschwind kommen Sie, lassen Sie uns den Rechten suchen.
DER WIRT. Ist es nicht der Rechte? Ei ja doch!
FRANZISKA. Ei nicht doch! Geschwind kommen Sie! Ich habe Ihrer Jungfer Tochter noch keinen guten Morgen gesagt.

der 'tsvaitə dɛktə dən ʃlaiər 'tsuː
ʔʊnt keːrtə zɪç 'ʔap ʔʊnt 'vaintə daːtsuːː
„'ʔax, das duː liːkst ʔauf dər 'toːtənbaːr!
ʔɪç haːp dɪç gə'liːbət zoˑ 'mançəs 'jaːr."
dər 'drɪtə 'huːp ʔiːn viːdər zoˑ'glaiç
ʔʊnt 'kʏstə ziː ʔan dən 'mʊnt zoˑ 'blaiç:
„dɪç 'liːpt ʔɪç 'ʔɪmər, dɪç 'liːp ʔɪç¹ nɔx 'hɔyt
ʔʊnt 'veːrdə dɪç 'liːbən ʔɪn "ʔeːvɪçkait."
          ʔuːlant.

(Gesprächston; verschiedene Grade der Bewegung.)

fɔn 'tɛlhaim.   'ʔaː! mainə 'mɪna! —

das 'frɔylain.   'ʔaː! main 'tɛlhaim! —

fɔn 'tɛlhaim.   fɛr'tsaiən ziː, gnɛːdɪgəs 'frɔylain, — das frɔylain fɔn "barnhɛlm hiːr tsuˑ fɪndən —

das 'frɔylain. kan (ʔ)iːnən dɔx zoˑ 'gaːr ʔʊnʔɛr'vartət nɪçt zain? — ʔɪç zɔl (ʔ)iːnən fɛr'tsaiən, das (ʔ)ɪç nɔx (ʔ)iːrə 'mɪnaː bɪn? fɛrtsai'(ʔ)iːnən dər 'hɪməl, das (ʔ)ɪç nɔx das frɔylain fɔn 'barnhɛlm bɪn! —

fɔn 'tɛlhaim. gnɛːdɪgəs 'frɔylain —

das 'frɔylain. main 'her —

fɔn 'tɛlhaim. vɛn viːr ʔʊns 'baidərzaits nɪçt "ʔɪrən —

fran'tsɪskaː. 'jeː, her vɪrt, veːn 'brɪŋən ziˑ (ʔ)ʊns den daːʔ gə'ʃvɪnt 'kɔmən ziː, lasən ziˑ (ʔ)ʊns dən 'rɛçtən zuːxən.

dər 'vɪrt. ʔɪst es 'nɪçt dər rɛçtə? ʔai 'jaː dɔx!

fran'tsɪskaː. ʔai 'nɪçt dɔx! gə'ʃvɪnt 'kɔmən ziːː! ʔɪç haːbə (ʔ)iːrər jʊŋfər 'tɔxtər nɔx kainən guːtən 'mɔrgən gəzaːkt.

---

¹ Oder: ['liːb-ɪç].

DER WIRT. O! viel Ehre —
FRANZISKA. Kommen Sie, wir wollen den
Kuchenzettel machen. — Lassen Sie sehen, was
wir haben werden —
DER WIRT. Sie sollen haben; fürs erste —
FRANZISKA. Still, ja stille! Wenn das Fräulein
jetzt schon weiß, was sie zu Mittag speisen soll,
so ist es um ihren Appetit geschehen. Kommen
Sie, das müssen Sie mir allein sagen.
LESSING, *Minna von Barnhelm.*

Jetzt war es entschieden, kein Zweifel mehr
möglich, Fink hatte das Buch. Die braunen Bänder
rauschten auseinander, die Partei glich einem
Schwarm entsetzter Küchlein, unter welche der
Habicht stößt. Nur Lenore nahm sich zusammen
und trat entschlossen auf Fink zu. „Sie haben das
Buch, Herr von Fink, eine meiner Freundinnen
hat es verloren und ist sehr unglücklich darüber.
Sein Inhalt ist nicht für fremde Augen, er kann
in dieser Gesellschaft großen Ärger verursachen.
Ich bitte, daß Sie mir das Buch zurückgeben."

„Ein Buch?" frug Fink neugierig, „was für
ein Buch?"

„Verstellen Sie sich nicht", sagte Lenore, „es
ist uns allen deutlich, daß Sie es haben. Ich
kann nicht glauben, daß Sie es nach dem, was
ich Ihnen über die Folgen gesagt habe, noch einen
Augenblick behalten können."

„Ich könnte es behalten", nickte Fink. „Sie

dər 'vɪrt. ʔoː! 'fiːl 'ʔeːrə —

fran'tsɪskaː. 'komən ziː, viːr volən dən 'kɪçəntsɛtəl maxən. — lasən ziˑ zeːən, vas viːr 'haːbən veːrdən —

dər 'vɪrt. ziˑ zolən 'haːbən; fyːrs 'ʔeːrstə —

fran'tsɪskaː. 'ʃtɪl, 'jaː 'ʃtɪlə! vɛn das fröylain 'jɛtst ʃoːn vais, vas ziˑ tsuˑ 'mɪtak ʃpaizən zol, zoː ɪst əs ʊm iːrən (ʔ)apə'tiːt gə'ʃeːən. 'komən ziː, das mʏsən ziˑ (')miːr ʔa'lain zaːgən.

"lɛsɪŋ, 'mɪnaː fon "barnhɛlm.

(Erzählung und Gespräch; unbefangen, z T. lebhaft)

jɛtst vaːr əs ʔɛnt'ʃiːdən, kain 'tsvaifəl meːr məːklɪç, 'fɪŋk 'hatə das buːx. diˑ braunən 'bɛndər rauʃtən ʔausʔai'nandər, diˑ paʀ'tai glɪç (ʔ)ainəm ʃvarm ʔɛnt'zɛtstər 'kyːçlain. ʔʊntər velçə dər 'haːbɪçt ʃtəːst. nuːr lə'noːrə naːm zɪç tsu'zamən ʔʊnt traːt ʔɛnt'ʃlosən ʔauf fɪŋk 'tsuː. „'ziː 'haːbən das buːx, her fon 'fɪŋk, ʔainə mainər 'fröyndmən hat əs fɛr'loːrən ʔʊnt (ʔ)ɪst zeːr 'ʔʊnglʏklɪç daʀy:bər. zain 'ʔɪmhalt (ʔ)ɪst nɪçt fyːr 'frɛmdə ʔaugən, ʔɛr kan (ʔ)ɪn diːzər gə'zɛlʃaft groːsən 'ʔɛrgər fɛrʔuːrzaxən. ʔɪç 'bɪtə, das ziˑ miːr das buːx tsu'rʏkgeːbən."

„ʔain 'buːx?" fruːk 'fɪŋk 'nöygiːrɪç, „'vas fyːr (ʔ)ain buːx?"

„fɛr'ʃtelən ziˑ zɪç nɪçt," zaːktə lə'noːrə, „ʔɛs ɪst (ʔ)uns 'ʔalən 'döytlɪç, das ziˑ əs 'haːbən. ʔɪç kan nɪçt 'glaubən, das ziˑ əs naːx 'deːm, vas ɪç (ʔ)iːnən 'ʔyːbər diˑ 'folgən gəzaːkt haːbə, nox (ʔ)ainən 'ʔaugənblɪk bə'haltən kɵnən.

„ʔɪç 'kɵntə əs bəhaltən," nɪktə 'fɪŋk. „zi zɪnt

sind zu gütig, wenn Sie mir ein solches Zartgefühl zutrauen."

„Das wäre mehr als unartig", rief Lenore.

„Es würde mir das größte Vergnügen machen, mehr als unartig zu sein, wenn ich das Buch hätte. Ein Buch, das Ihnen oder einer Ihrer Freundinnen gehört, das möglicherweise Ihre Handschrift oder eine andere Erinnerung an Sie enthält, das werde ich Ihnen in keinem Fall zurückgeben, wenn ich es finde; und wenn ich erfahre, wo es liegt, werde ich es stehlen. Und wenn ich es habe, werde ich es Zeile für Zeile auswendig lernen. Ich werde Ihnen dadurch zu gefallen suchen, daß ich Ihnen einige Stellen daraus vortrage, so oft ich die Freude habe, Sie zu sehen."

Lenore trat ihm einen Schritt näher, und ihre Augen flammten. „Wenn Sie das tun, Herr von Fink", rief sie, „so werden Sie als ein Unwürdiger handeln."

Fink nickte ihr freundlich zu. „Der Eifer steht Ihnen allerliebst, Fräulein; aber wie können Sie Würde von einem lustigen Vogel verlangen, wie ich bin? Die Natur hat ihre Gaben verschieden ausgeteilt; manchem hat sie verliehen, Verse zu machen, andere zeichnen kleine Bilder, ich habe von ihr einen spitzen Schnabel erhalten, den gebrauche ich. Haben Sie je einen würdigen Zeisig gesehen?" Er wandte sich lachend ab, faßte Benno Tönnchen beim Arm und ging mit ihm nach der Tür.

G. FREYTAG, *Soll und Haben.*

tsu 'gyːtɪç, vɛn ziˑ miːr (ʔ)ain zɔlçəs 'tsaːrtgəfyːl tsuːtrauən."

„das vɛːrə 'meːr (ʔ)als "ʔʊnʔaːrtɪç," riːf leˑ'noːrə.

„ʔɛs vʏrdə miːr das 'greːstə fɛr'gnyːgən maxən, 'meːr (ʔ)als 'ʔʊnʔaːrtɪç tsu zain, vɛn ɪç das buːx 'hɛtə. ʔain 'buːx, das 'ʔiːnən ʔoːdər ʔainər ʔiːrər 'frɔyndɪnən gəheːrt, das 'meːklɪçər 'vaizə 'ʔiːrə 'hantʃrɪft ʔoːdər ʔainə 'ʔandərə ʔɛr'ʔɪnəruŋ ʔan 'ziː ʔɛnthɛlt, das veːrdə ɪç (ʔ)iːnən (ʔ)ɪn 'kainəm 'fal tsu'rʏkgeːbən, vɛn ɪç əs 'fɪndə; ʔʊnt vɛn ɪç (ʔ)ɛr'faːrə, voː əs 'liːkt, veːrdə ɪç əs 'ʃteːlən. ʔʊnt vɛn ɪç əs 'haːbə, veːrdə ɪç əs 'tsailə fyːr 'tsailə 'ʔausvɛndɪç lɛrnən. ʔɪç veːrdə (ʔ)iːnən daːdʊrç tsuˑ gə'falən zuːxən, das ɪç (ʔ)iːnən, (ʔ)ainɪgə 'ʃtɛlən daːraus 'foːrtraːgə, zoˑ 'ʔɔft ɪç diˑ 'frɔydə haːbə, ziː tsuˑ 'zeːən."

leˑ'noːrə traːt (ʔ)iːm (ʔ)ainən ʃrɪt 'nɛːər, ʔʊnt (ʔ)iːrə 'ʔaugən 'flamtən. „(')vɛn ziˑ 'das 'tuːn, hɛr fɔn 'fɪŋk", 'riːf ziː, „zoˑ veːrdən ziˑ (ʔ)als ʔain 'ʔʊnvʏrdɪgər handəln."

'fɪŋk nɪktə (ʔ)iːr frɔyntlɪç 'tsuː. „deːr 'ʔaifər ʃteːt (ʔ)iːnən ʔalər'liːpst, 'frɔylain; ʔaːbər viː kɔnən ziˑ 'vʏrdə fɔn (ʔ)ainəm lʊstɪgən 'foːgəl fɛrlaŋən, viˑ 'ʔɪç bɪn? diˑ na'tuːr hat (ʔ)iːrə gaːbən fɛr'ʃiːdən ʔausgətailt; 'mançəm hat ziˑ fɛrliːən, 'fɛrzə tsuˑ maxən, 'ʔandərə tsaiçnən klainə 'bɪldər, 'ʔɪç haːbə fɔn (ʔ)iːr (ʔ)ainən ʃpɪtsən 'ʃnaːbəl ʔɛrhaltən, deːn gə'brauxə (ʔ)ɪç. haːbən ziˑ jeː (ʔ)ainən 'vʏrdɪgən 'tsaizɪç gəzeːən?" ʔeːr (')vantə zɪç 'laxənt 'ʔap, (')fastə 'bɛnoː 'tənçən baim 'ʔarm ʔʊnt (')gɪŋ mɪt (ʔ ,iːm naːx dər 'tyːr.

'geː ('gʊstaːf) "fraitaːk, 'zɔl ʔʊnt "haːbən.

BIBLIOLIFE

Old Books Deserve a New Life
www.bibliolife.com

Did you know that you can get most of our titles in our trademark **EasyScript**[TM] print format? **EasyScript**[TM] provides readers with a larger than average typeface, for a reading experience that's easier on the eyes.

Did you know that we have an ever-growing collection of books in many languages?

Order online:
www.bibliolife.com/store

Or to exclusively browse our **EasyScript**[TM] collection:
www.bibliogrande.com

At BiblioLife, we aim to make knowledge more accessible by making thousands of titles available to you – quickly and affordably.

Contact us:
BiblioLife
PO Box 21206
Charleston, SC 29413

Lightning Source UK Ltd.
Milton Keynes UK
02 October 2009

144448UK00001B/7/A